THE WORLD'S
ALIEN ENCOUNTERS

Photograph Acknowledgements

Fortean Picture Library 7, 10, 11, 14, 15 top, 15 bottom, 16, 19, 21, 23, 30 top, 30 bottom, 47, 48, 50 top, 53, 54, 62, 102, 103, 121, 124, 130/Peter Brookesmith 80 bottom/Seale Photography 81/Dennis Stacy 55, 56 top, 56 bottom, 80 top, 88, 146, 150/Deszö Sternoczky/SUFOI 50 bottom, 119

THE WORLD'S GREATEST
ALIEN ENCOUNTERS

Nigel Cawthorne

CHANCELLOR
PRESS

This 2002 edition published by Chancellor Press,
an imprint of Bounty Books, a division of
Octopus Publishing Group Ltd.,
2–4 Heron Quays, London E14 4JP

Reprinted 2002

ISBN 0 7537 0564 8

A CIP catalogue record for this book is available from
the British Library

Printed in England by Mackays of Chatham

Contents

1 Close Encounters of the Third Kind

Adamski

In ancient times, humans had contact with beings that came down from the heavens. But the first well-documented contactee of modern times – that is, since the age of the flying saucer which began in 1947 – was a Polish American named George Adamski, who chronicled his adventures with the 'space people' in several books. A self-made man with interests in astronomy and oriental philosophies, Adamski took six friends out on a picnic in the Mojave Desert in California on 20 November 1952.

UFO contactee George Adamski (left) being interviewed on American television by Long John Nebel.

The purpose of the expedition was to spot and photograph flying saucers. They were not disappointed. Shortly after a light lunch, a gigantic cigar-shaped craft glided silently into view. It was chased away by military jets – but not before it had ejected a silver disc which landed some distance away. Adamski and two of his friends drove off into the desert after it, hoping to get a closer view and perhaps even take some photographs. At the end of a dirt road, they stopped. Adamski set up his tripod-mounted portable telescope and took a number of photographs of the silvery craft through it. Then he ventured alone out into the desert to get some close-ups.

Before he reached it, the alien craft shot skywards and soared out into space. A few minutes later, a second, smaller, saucer-shaped craft appeared. It was gliding between two mountain peaks some way ahead of Adamski. He watched and photographed the craft as it landed about four hundred yards away. A figure got out and beckoned to him. At first Adamski thought the figure was a man.

'But the beauty of his form surpassed anything I had ever seen,' Adamski recalled later. The humanoid was short, about 5 feet 3 inches. He had smooth, tanned skin and long blond hair, and he was dressed in a brown one-piece suit with a broad belt, and red shoes. Adamski put out his hand to shake hands with the being, who was plainly familiar with the gesture. But when palm-to-palm contact was established, the two began communicating using telepathy, though sign language was needed to clarify some points. The creature's name was Orthon. He came from Venus, where he and his fellow Venusians lived a pure, spiritual and God-fearing way of life. He had come to Earth, he said, to warn humankind about the dangers of nuclear energy and pollution. He refused to be photographed, then stepped into his craft and shot off back into space. First contact had been made. There were no photographs of the alien, but the encounter had been witnessed by Adamski's friends, who had been standing a few hundred yards away.

George Adamski had been born in Poland on 17 April 1891. In 1893, he emigrated to New York with his family. In 1913 he joined the US Army, serving in 13th US Cavalry, K Troop, until 1916. In 1918 worked as a government painter and decorator at the Yellowstone National Park. He also served with the National Guard, stationed at Portland, Oregon, and received an honourable discharge in 1919.

After that, things get a bit murky. It is now thought that, during Prohibition, which began in 1920, Adamski worked as a bootleg-ger. In 1926 he settled at Laguna, California, where he began lec-turing on oriental philosophy, though he had no formal training. In 1940 he moved to Valley Center, California, where he established a cult movement known as the Royal Order of Tibet. As its spiritu-al leader, Adamski became a self-styled professor of philosophy. It was there, on 9 October 1946, that Adamski claimed to have seen a 'dirigible-shaped mother ship' flying over his home, a full nine months before Kenneth Arnold's legendary flying saucer sighting. It was a sign. Adamski took his followers on a trek across California. The cult settled on the southern slopes of Mount Palomar, famous for the astronomical observatory that sits on its peak. From there, he set out to make contact with the aliens that were plainly visiting the Earth. Soon, the quietly spoken Polish immigrant achieved world-wide celebrity status as the world's first alien contactee.

The incredible tale of the world's first face-to-face extraterres-tial encounter is recounted at great length by Adamski in *Flying Saucers Have Landed* in 1953. It was the first of many meetings with Venusians. Adamski lectured widely and his cult following grew. Those who came to hear him were told of strange journeys to distant worlds. The Venusians had taken him home to Venus and, with them, he had visited the Moon and Mars. He supported his claims with photographs of alien craft allegedly taken through his telescope. A month after his first alien contact, he photographed a 'Venusian scout craft', thirty-five feet in diameter, hovering above his home in Palomar Gardens, California. And in 1951 Adamski snapped the cigar-shaped 'mother ship' hovering there, ready to take him on an interplanetary jaunt. He also supplied detailed drawings of the interior. The newspapers around the world lapped it up. And Adamski was widely billed as a professor from the Palomar Observatory, which was not altogether untrue. Before he came to fame, he ran a hot dog stall in its grounds.

When *Flying Saucers Have Landed* was published in 1953, it became an instant best-seller. Two years later his new adventures reached a world audience with *Inside the Flying Saucers*. This recounts his experiences on board the Venusians' ship, another first in UFOlogy. The reader is given a fascinating account of what it is like to travel though space, and Adamski describes in great detail life on the still-to-be-explored Moon. There were forests, lakes, wooded valleys and snow-covered mountains on the lunar land-

UFO contactee George Adamski with his six-inch telescope on Mount Palomar, California, USA.

scape, and citizens of the Moon 'strolled down the sidewalks' in lunar cities, just as humans did in Earth cities, he said. The aliens also informed Adamski that the Earth was being visited by beings from the solar system and beyond.

Some dismissed his tales of planetary excursions as the ramblings of a troubled mind. Nevertheless, he managed to attract a band of illustrious supporters. *Flying Saucers Have Landed* was co-written by Desmond Leslie the British author, Winston Churchill's cousin. He was dubbed the 'Saucerer Royal'. Queen Juliana of the Netherlands received Adamski at her palace in Amsterdam and it was said that Pope John XXIII granted him a private audience on 31 May 1963 – though the Vatican has denied the claim.

After one of Adamski's trips into space, two people who had witnessed his departure through binoculars signed affidavits backing his story. In an effort to discredit Adamski, UFO researcher Thomas Eickhoff tried to sue in the Federal Court so that he would get an opportunity to cross-examine them. The US government blocked the case. This was no accident, Adamski said. Washington sanctioned his efforts. Indeed, document requests under the Freedom of Information Act show that Adamski was in contact with the FBI. They contacted him to warn him to stop 'inferring that the FBI cleared his material on space travel'. Other FBI memos denounce Adamski as a Communist and say that he was 'mentally disturbed'.

In his defence, even sceptics were impressed with Adamski's apparent sincerity. Science journalist Robert Chapman wrote of a meeting with the great man in *UFO – Flying Saucers Over Britain*, 'Adamski was so damnably normal and this was the overall impression I carried away. He believed he had made contact with a man from Venus, and he did not see why anyone should disbelieve him. I told myself that if he was deluded he was the most lucid and intelligent man I had met.'

Adamski's third book, *Flying Saucer Farewell*, was published in 1961. But, by then, he was being greeted by a more educated and sceptical audience. On 12 September 1959 the Soviets had managed to hit the moon with their probe Luna 2 and, on 4 October 1959, Luna 3 orbited the moon and sent back pictures of the far side. There were no forests, lakes, wooded valleys and snow-capped mountains to seen. Nor were there any cities. The lunar surface was a barren stretch of rocks, dust and craters. When asked to explain this, Adamski accused the Soviets of falsifying the pictures to deceive the Americans.

UFO contactee George Adamski.

Adamski died on 23 April 1965, aged 73, as a series of new probes, both Soviet and American, were heading for the moon to further undermine his story. At best, it can be said that Adamski made wild exaggerations, which certainly destroyed any reputation he may have had. Today, he is largely dismissed as a fraud. However, when he died he left behind a huge collection of photographs and film footage, much of which has still not been discredited. True his photographs of 'mother ships' and their 'scout craft' may be seem too good to be true. Critics have compared them variously to part of a vacuum cleaner, a chicken feeder and a bottle cooling machine made in Wigan, Lancashire, which intriguingly turned out to have been designed after the photographs were released. But while sceptics have mocked them, no one has proved them to be fakes.

On 26 February 1965, just months before he died, Adamski was staying with the Rodeffers at their house in Silver Spring, Maryland. That afternoon, Adamski and Madeleine Rodeffer saw something hovering through some trees. A car drew up and three men told Adamski: 'Get your cameras – they're here.' Then they drove off. Adamski grabbed the Rodeffers' cine camera and produced some 8mm colour footage which is among with most convincing UFO footage ever. Despite rigorous analysis, this film has stood the test of time.

NASA claims that the film shows a three-foot model. However, Adamski was neither an accomplished model maker, nor was he well-versed in special effects. Optical physicist William T. Sherwood, former project development engineer for Eastman-Kodak, spent a great deal of time examining the film and found that it had not been tampered with. The image, he says, shows a craft around twenty-five feet across. As it flies through the frames, it becomes distorted. Veteran aeronautics engineer Leonard Cramp says that this was caused by a powerful gravitational field produced by the craft.

Others around the world who had never heard of Adamski have sighted identical objects to the craft the film depicts. One of them was a schoolboy named Stephen Darbishire who, with his cousin, took two photographs in Coniston, Lancashire one day in February 1954. Cramp used a technique called orthographic projection to prove that the object depicted in Darbishire's and Adamski's photographs were proportionally identical.

Prominent UFOlogist Nick Pope also believes that Adamski's film is authentic and refuses to dismiss Adamski.

'My own intensive investigations over several decades have led me to the conviction that, even if some of his claims are nonsensical, others are legitimate,' Pope says. And he has other reputable backers. Adamski was the first to claim that contact had been established, at a 'restricted' level, between the Venusians and the scientific community, and the aliens were providing assistance in the space programme. This was confirmed by Dr Hermann Oberth, a senior rocket scientist who worked with NASA in the late 1950s.

There is other high-powered corroboration. On his first trip into space, Adamski said he observed 'manifestations taking place all around us, as though billions upon billions of fireflies were flickering everywhere'. This is not something that would readily emerge from the imagination to be included in a space yarn. When US astronaut John Glenn became the first American to orbit Earth on 20 February 1962, he said: 'A lot of the little things I thought were stars were actually a bright yellowish green about the size and intensity as looking at a firefly on a real dark night... there were literally thousands of them.' Russian cosmonauts have seen the same thing. They turned out to be billions of reflective dust particles. How could George Adamski have known?

Welcome to the Universal Confederation

After Adamski, aliens seemed to be queuing up to chat to humans. They first contacted Richard Miller by short-wave radio in 1954. They told him to go to an isolated place near Ann Arbor in Michigan, where after fifteen minutes a disc-shaped craft appeared and landed nearby. This spaceship, he learned later, was called 'Phoenix'. A doorway opened in the base of the vehicle and a staircase descended.

A young humanoid dressed in a brown one-piece space suit stood at the top of the stairs. He beckoned Miller to enter the ship, which he did. He found himself was standing in a large hallway which seemed to encircle the whole craft. The alien said nothing but the creature radiated a kind of friendliness that put him at his ease.

Miller was taken to the control room of the ship where he met the alien commander. His name was Soltec and he greeted Miller in perfect English. He explained that their home planet was Centurus of the Alpha Centauri system. It belonged to the 'Universal Confederation', a group of some 680 planets which earned the right to membership by their evolutionary progress.

Miller was told that, before Earth could become a member, mankind would have to awaken to higher spiritual values.

'When love of your fellow man becomes established, then will the "Sons of Light" appear and the Kingdom of your God will reign on Earth,' Miller was told. The 'Sons of Light', it was explained, were what the Bible called 'angels'.

Richard Miller's contacts with the extraterrestrials continued for over twenty years and he meticulously recorded all his contacts in a library of writings and tapes.

Independence Day

In 1954 Daniel Fry, a scientist at the White Sands Missile Range in New Mexico, claimed that he had been in contact with aliens for some time. On 4 July Fry missed the bus taking employees into town to see the Independence Day fireworks display and decided instead to take a walk in the desert to enjoy the cool night air. As he looked up he noticed that the stars were being blocked out by something descending.

Dan Fry.

It was a metallic object, oblate spheroid in shape, and it landed on the desert floor about seventy feet away from him. He approached the sphere, and heard a voice warning him not to touch the craft as the hull was still extremely hot. Fry was so shocked he fell over a root, and the voice attempted to calm him. According to Fry, the alien was up to speed on all the latest American slang. The voice belonged to an extraterrestrial called 'A-Lan' who was communicating with him telepathically. He had come to Earth to collect air samples.

A-Lan invited Fry to enter the ship. Once he was on board the craft took off and travelled to New York City and back in half-an-hour. This would have meant that it was travelling at a speed of over eight thousand miles an hour, yet Fry felt nothing except a slight motion. He was released back into the desert with the promise that there would be further contacts. Fry was given the task of preaching the aliens' philosophy of understanding to human society. A-Lan claimed that his race were the descendants of a previous Earth civilisation that had emigrated into space thirty thousand years ago.

Fry produced clear daylight photographs of the UFO to support his story. One, taken in 1965, shows two alien spacecraft hovering over a Joshua tree in California. He also founded a quasi-religious group called 'Understanding' to pass on the words of A-Lan. He published his claims in a book, which came out shortly after Adamski's. This gave him high-profile media coverage and earned him vociferous public support. However, he agreed to take a lie detector test live on television and appeared to fail – though the results are

UFO photographed by Daniel Fry, UFO contactee.

UFO photographed by Dan Fry at Merlin, Oregon, USA, in May 1964.

open to debate. But it is difficult to dismiss him as a hoaxer. As a scientist with a well-paid job, he risked destroying his career.

Like Adamski, Fry and a number of high-profile contactees said that the aliens that had spoken to them had come to warn humankind about the proliferation of nuclear weapons. After the Soviet Union exploded its first atomic bomb in 1949, this was plainly a concern to everyone on the planet. The beginnings of the space race also focused mankind's attention on the mysteries of the universe.

Hoaxers?

Many early contactees were completely discredited both by scientists and UFOlogists, eager to winnow out hoaxes. Dr J. Allen Hynek, scientific consultant to Project Blue Book – the US military's UFO monitor – denounced the early wave of contactees as 'pseudo-religious fanatics' of 'low credibility value'. Nevertheless many contactees enjoyed celebrity status.

Dr. J. Allen Hynek.

In 1962, after being interviewed by the Air Ministry, fourteen-year-old British schoolboy Alex Birch became a minor celebrity on TV, radio and the lecture circuit after photographing five saucer-like craft. Ten years later, Birch admitted that the photographs had been faked. After that, Britain's UFO Research Organisation laid down guidelines for assessing photographic evidence. All negatives had to be submitted, along with the original film. Pictures should contain other objects, such as houses or trees, as a point of reference so estimates of size and distance could be made. Ideally, there should be an independent eyewitness to any encounter.

Despite his official role, even Hynek conceded that some UFO encounters were genuine. Twenty-three per cent of Project Blue

Book's sightings – which ran from 1951 to 1969 – remain unexplained. He went on to found the Center for UFO Studies in 1973.

Danger UFO

Not all contact was benign. On 20 May 1967, Stephen Michalak saw a UFO land at Falcon Lake in the US. He managed to get close enough to touch it. As he did so, he said that a burst of intense light came blasting out of one of the spacecraft's 'exhaust panels', setting his shirt on fire and giving him first-degree burns. An investigation of the landing site found fragments of silver that had been exposed to great heat and a high level of radioactivity.

After his encounter, Michalak became ill. He suffered from dizziness, nausea, swollen joints and skin infections. In an effort of get his condition diagnosed, he visited twenty-seven doctors. None of them offered an explanation for his ill health.

Supplies from the Skies

Some aliens come to Earth for more down-to-earth reasons. One such visited Joe Simonton, a farmer, on the morning of 18 April 1961. Simonton noticed a bright, saucer-shaped object land near his farmhouse in Eagle River, Wisconsin, and went to check it out. It was about thirty feet across and twelve feet high. To his astonishment, a hatch opened and an alien climbed out. The figure was humanoid, about five feet tall and dressed like a human. The alien had no great message to communicate. Instead he waved an empty jug about. Simonton took this to mean that he wanted water and went to fetch it. When he returned, he found that the hospitable alien had set up a barbecue inside the craft and was cooking. The alien gave Simonton a 'pancake' in return for the water, then the alien closed the hatch and flew away. The pancake was analysed by a US Food and Drug Administration laboratory. No extraterrestrial ingredients were found, though there was a distinct absence of salt.

Pit Stop

On 24 April 1950 Bruno Facchini saw sparks near his home in

Abbiate Buazzone, in Italy. At first he thought they were being generated by a storm, but when he went outside to investigate, he saw a dark UFO hovering just above the ground some two hundred yards away.

Nearby, a figure seemed to be working on the object, perhaps making repairs. Other entities were also seen near and around the object. They were dressed in tight-fitting clothes and were wearing helmets, but their faces were concealed behind masks that were connected to the craft by flexible pipes.

During the encounter, Facchini offered to help, but the entities fired a beam of light at him that blasted him along the ground for several yards. Shortly afterwards, when the repairs had apparently been completed, the object took off, making a heavy buzzing sound.

The following day Facchini returned to the site, where he found circular imprints and patches of scorched grass, and recovered metal fragments. There were a number of other witnesses to the event but they preferred to remain anonymous.

Contact Kentucky-style

One of the most famous alien contact stories occurred at Sutton Farm, Hopkinsville, Kentucky on the 21 August 1955.

At around 7 p.m., Billy Ray Taylor went out to fetch some water from the family well. While there, he noticed a large shining object land close to the farm. When he told the other family members inside the house they all laughed and failed to take him seriously.

Some time later, they heard their dog barking wildly outside, and Lucky and Billy went out to investigate. They had walked a few yards from the front door when they saw a small three-foot creature walking towards them. They described the creature as having large yellow eyes, a long thin mouth, large ears, thin short legs, and claws for hands.

One of the men then fired a shot from his .22 rifle. The creature, obviously hit, ran quickly into the woods.

When the men returned home – but before they had a chance to tell their incredible story – the house came under siege by a group of similar looking creatures. The eight adults and three children in the house at the time were all terrified as creature after creature appeared at windows around the house and the men loosed off another round whenever they got a clear shot at a creature.

The siege lasted around two hours before the family decided to make a run for the family pickup truck. They drove down to the local police station to report the event. When police officers turned up at the farm they could find no evidence of the strange creatures. However, there were gunshot holes in the windows and walls.

Police officers later admitted to seeing strange lights coming from the vicinity of the Sutton farm, but they did not bother to report them at the time.

Many people believe this to be a complete hoax. But the family made no money from the incident and shunned publicity. They had to make extensive repairs to the house, which cost a considerable amount of money. And all eight witnesses told the same story.

Alpine Encounters

Some bizarre stories have been told by those who have been visited by extraterrestrials, but none can match that related by the one-armed Swiss farmer Eduard 'Billy' Meier. Throughout the 1970s and 1980s he was in regular contact with the 'Pleiadians', as his alien contacts were called, who visited from a far-off galaxy. They not only passed on their all their secrets and whisked him around the universe, they took him back in time to meet Jesus and into a mystical realm where he photographed the 'Eye of God'. Despite his outlandish claims, Meier could back what he said with the most comprehensive body of evidence any contactee has ever come up with. He had a thousand photographs of his many meetings with aliens and

Eduard 'Billy' Mier.

twelve films of alien spaceships. He also logged his conversations with the visitors and had reams of notes on the technical and spiritual knowledge passed to him by the Pleiadians. He also had a variety of mineral and rock samples, and over forty independent eye-witnesses said that they had seen him make contact with alien spaceships.

This huge body of evidence made Meier's story a landmark case in UFO history. It split the UFO lobby in two. Those who saw him as a fake attacked him with unprecedented hostility. But his supporters remain vehement in his defence.

Meier probably had his first encounter with UFOs in 1975, when he was a happily married man and the father of three children. They appeared to him in the woods behind his farm in Hinwil. But later, he recalled that when he was five, he saw a 'large circular craft' flying over the local church. For some reason, the aliens had picked him out as their chosen contact on Earth. Soon afterwards, he started receiving telepathic messages from the extraterrestrials. They urged him to mug up as much as he possible on the Earth's various religions and prepare himself for later visitations.

This preparation took Meier to many unusual places. He travelled extensively through Europe and India. He supported his quest by working as racing car driver and a snake charmer. He also spent time in the French Foreign Legion and, during his time as an industrial worker, he lost an arm in an accident. His travels exposed Meier to many different ways of life, broadening his mind and preparing him spiritually. 'His soul could understand ideas communicated to him better than our souls could,' says one supporter.

By the mid-1970s he was plainly ready. Between 1975 and 1978, he had over 130 well-documented meetings with visitors from the Pleiades, a cluster of stars about four hundred light years from Earth. The contacts followed a set pattern. Meier would feel a gentle breeze on his forehead, then he would receive telepathic instructions telling him where the starship would be landing. The meetings would begin with a photo call. Normally the aliens' spacecraft were invisible, but for the purposes of terrestrial photography they would be made visible by generating special cloaks of visibility around them. The Pleiadians made their craft visible and encouraged him to take photographs so that he had evidence of their meetings. He had pictures of numerous different types of craft, demonstrating the wide range of their technology.

During the 1970s, Eduard 'Billy' Mier of Switzerland claimed contacts with people from Pleiades and photographed many of their UFOs/spacecraft.

Encounters would usually take place in various spots around southeast Zurich. He was invited to bring friends along, though they were never actually allowed to meet the Pleiadians. However, a number of them testified to seeing the lights of the visiting craft at dusk or dawn. After the initial photo session was over, Meier was transported instantly on board the alien craft. Some of his friends saw him beamed on board. They also photographed the landing sites after Meier's meetings, showing the marks of the alien craft in the grass.

During his many lengthy conversations with the Pleiadians, Meier discovered that they came from a planet called Erra, which had a population of some 127 billion. Pleiadians were similar to humans but, 'benefiting from greater time, and greater knowledge', they boasted that their civilisation was some three thousand years ahead of ours. They had come to Earth to make humankind aware of extraterrestrial life. And they told Meier that he and other contactees had been selected as the conduit for this knowledge. The Pleiadians picked candidates for contact using the technology that recorded 'soul patterns' they had developed. This had led the Pleiadians to choose Meier as their principal contact.

The Pleiadian Meier met most often was a female named Semjase. He first met her on 28 January 1978. Although she was 344 years old, she was pretty and had smooth fair skin – not a wrinkle in sight, apparently. From the photograph Meier took of her, she seems indistinguishable from an Earth woman, though she had with slightly longer earlobes. On her home planet of Erra, she was considered a demi-goddess and had learnt a lot about Earth from her father, 770-year-old Ptaah. He held the title 'King of Wisdom', and ruled over three inhabited planets, including Earth, dispensing help and advice when it was needed. It was Semjase's grandfather Sfath who had first made contact with Meier in 1942. Sfath had come to Earth in a silver spacecraft and taken the five-year-old Meier for a flight on board. He also educated Meier in Pleiadian ways through the medium of telepathy.

While most contactees had little in the way of evidence to support their claims, Meier had a surfeit of it. To some, this alone was suspicious, and they claimed that Meier had pulled off an impressive hoax. Others claimed that Meier was the butt of a bitter campaign to discredit him. They formed themselves into a support group called Genesis III. A leading member is retired US Air Force colonel Wendelle Stevens, who maintains that Meier's story was not a hoax and his evidence is impressive.

'The pictures were super fantastic,' Stevens says. 'I had never seen anything like them before.'

The book *Light Years* details Gary Kinder's three-year investigation of the Meier case. Kinder is convinced of the authenticity of Meier's photographs, films, sound recordings and the mineral samples given to Meier by a Pleiadian astronaut called Quetzel. Analysis of the soundtrack recording of a Pleiadian 'beamship' – made while it was hovering invisibly – proved conclusive to Kinder's ears. Quetzel's mineral samples were handed over to the scientist Dr Marcel Vogel for analysis. Most were of perfectly ordi-

During the 1970s, Eduard Billy Meier of Switzerland claimed contacts
with people from Pleiades and photographed many of their UFOs/spacecraft.

nary terrestrial material, though one possessed properties that were
'not immediately explainable'. It must be said that producing the
number of models required to fake all the photographs would be
difficult for a one-armed man and would have cost large sums of
money – far beyond the means of a poor farmer. Kinder says that
if Meier is not telling the truth, then he must be one of the finest
illusionists the world has ever known.

Another investigator, Kal Korff, is convinced that this is the case
and calls Meier story 'the most infamous hoax in UFOlogy' and set
about trashing the photographic evidence. Stevens and Genesis III
claimed that Meier's photographs had been subjected to computer
analysis, which proved that they had not been tampered with and
no 'paste-ups' or double exposures were used. But that did not rule
out the use of models. Indeed Meier admitted making models of the
Pleiadan craft he had seen, but only as an aide memoire.

Korff points out that, in the photographs, the shadows on the
saucers rarely matched those on the landscapes. Often the craft
were in too sharp focus to have been photographed in front of a real

landscape. Many of them are at exactly the same angle to the camera, though Meier claimed to have taken them at different times and in different places. One photograph shows a Swiss fighter aircraft in the background, but the pilot had no recollection of seeing a UFO. In 8mm colour film of one of Meier's meetings, an alien craft is shown coming to a halt. As it does so, it wobbles back and forth as if on a fishing line. Korff also interviewed Meier's wife Kaliope – also known as Popi – who supported her husband during the 1970s and 1980s. But following their divorce she now says that his photographs were fakes.

Korff presented his damning evidence in his book *Spaceships of the Pleiades*. This did such a good job in undermining Meier's credibility that most leading UFOlogists in Europe and America rejected him as a charlatan. As Meier's reputation declined, the Pleiadians took him off to ever more outlandish destinations. On a Pleiadian time machine, he travelled back to prehistoric times where he photographed a pterodactyl with a pyramid in the background and snapped the 'Eye of God', which, judging by the photo, was winking at the time. More recently, he met Muhammad and Jesus, who made him a disciple. He also travelled into the future and watched the San Andreas Fault open up and swallow San Francisco. The Pleiadians also gave him a 'laser gun' – though, sadly, he has not used it to zap his critics.

The Pleiadians also gave him their most precious gift of all – their wisdom. This amounted to little more than the teachings of Jesus and could by summed up as: 'Do unto others as you would have them do unto you.'

'It was a very basic wisdom,' scoffs Korff. But it was enough to win Meier a following in the New Age movement.

However, Meier's bizarre claims undermined his credibility further among UFOlogists. Astronomers say that all of the five hundred stars in the Pleiades cluster are fiercely hot and the chance of life surviving on planets orbiting them is negligible. Meier is now widely regarded as a hoaxer, though he still has more evidence to back his claims that any other contactee.

A Meeting in Mexico

It was Mexican photographer Carlos Diaz's lucky day, when early one January morning in 1981, he pulled into a deserted car park at the top of a hill, in Ajusco Park near Mexico City. He was on assignment for a magazine, and had arranged to meet a journalist there. The journalist had not turned up and as Diaz sat in his car and waited, he prepared his camera for the job.

He soon grew impatient. Even though it was early in the morning, humidity was already uncomfortable. Diaz began to look at his watch. But then he became conscious of a strange yellow glow. At first he thought it was a forest fire on the slopes below the car park. Then he saw a large, orange, oval UFO, rising up from the valley below. It stopped, hovering about thirty yards in front of his car.

Diaz knew a photo opportunity when he saw one. He grabbed his camera and, with it resting on the steering wheel, he began firing off shots. Suddenly the whole car began to shake violently. So Diaz leapt out of the vehicle, getting two more shots before the craft soared vertically into the sky. Three shots came out perfectly. His amazing pictures have been examined by a range of experts. All have concluded that they are genuine.

Mexico City had long been a UFO hotspot and Diaz's encounter was almost run-of-the-mill. But the sighting had made a profound effect on Diaz. He kept returning to Ajusco Park in the hope of getting more pictures. For two months, his visits were fruitless visits. But then, on 23 March, his tenacity was rewarded.

This time he went roaming through the forest. It was a foul night, but through the fog and rain, Diaz saw an orange glow. Scaling the walls of a valley, he managed to get within fifty yards of the object. The source of the bright orange light was a dome-shaped craft with a smooth ring around its middle. This was covered with a series of small domes, each around three feet in diameter.

Diaz hid behind some rocks to watch the craft. Suddenly, someone behind him grabbed him by the shoulder. Diaz passed out. When he awoke, it was dark and the mysterious craft was gone. Despite the heavy rain, he found that his clothes were completely dry. It was then that he realised something very strange had happened.

When he returned to his car, he found that he was not alone. A humanoid entity with fair hair was waiting for him. The creature told Diaz that if he wanted to know more about what had happened, he should come back at noon the next day. He did and the humanoid was sitting on the grass waiting for him. The being explained that he had come from inside the craft Diaz had seen and that it was he who had grabbed Diaz's shoulder the previous day. He said no more, but promised Diaz that he would gradually recover his memory of what had happened.

Over the next few months, Diaz's memory returned, little by little. He recalled that he had seen the craft hovering directly over his head. As he reached up to touch it, his hand passed through its yellow aura and he seemed to meld with it. Then he recalled seeing the craft parked on a platform inside a giant cave.

'It was full of stalagmites, some of which were carved into what appeared to be Mayan sculptures,' Diaz said. 'I saw many "people" in the cave, some of whom waved to me and, in a state of shock, I waved back.'

The humanoid Diaz had met in the park was with Diaz outside the cave and told him that his extraterrestrial race had strong connections with both the Mayan and Aztec civilisations, which they had been visiting for millennia. Indeed, Diaz's hometown, Tepoztlan, is named after Tepoztcom, the son of the Aztec god Quetzalcoatl who, according to legend, descended from the heavens to bring knowledge to the Aztec people. The area around Tepoztlan has been considered sacred for hundreds of years.

His alien contact then took Diaz to another smaller cave. This contained seven glowing, egg-shaped orbs. Diaz was invited to step into one of them. Inside, Diaz found himself bathed in yellow light. But then this turned into an image of a forest.

'I could see all the details of the forest as if I was walking through it,' Diaz said. 'I couldn't touch anything, but I could feel the temperature and moisture. I could see and experience everything, yet I wasn't physically there.'

According to his guide, these orbs were data storage systems. While he was inside, certain information had been imparted to him. Puzzling though this was, it was only the first of a series of contacts. Each time he was taken to the orbs. Inside he has 'travelled' to different regions of the Earth's ecosystem – forest, desert, jungle, shoreline and even Arctic areas. Through his alien contacts, Diaz has become deeply aware of the interconnectedness of all life and the need to protect the environment. These claims may appear far-fetched, but Diaz is considered a highly reliable source, and can back his claims with photographic evidence.

Mexican TV journalist and UFOlogist Jaime Maussan, who became a leading UFO investigator since the Mexican wave of sightings in 1991, came across Diaz's UFO photographs and says they are among the best he has seen. He took Diaz's photographs to Jim Dilettoso, an image-processing expert at Village Labs, in Tucson, Arizona, who ruled out any possibility of a hoax.

Maussan then gave the transparencies to Professor Victor Quesada at the Polytechnical Institute of the University of Mexico for examination.

'We were shocked to discover that the spectrum of light from the object was unlike anything we had ever seen,' said Professor Quesada. 'It broke all pervious parameters and did not match anything in out data banks. The light was extraordinarily intense. There was no evidence of superimposition or a hoax. We estimate the object to be around thirty to fifty metres in diameter.'

The photographs were also analysed by Dr Robert Nathan at NASA's Jet Propulsion Laboratory in Pasadena, California. A notorious UFO sceptic, Nathan admitted defeat. He could find no evidence of a fake. One picture, the first Diaz took, is the most impressive. It was shot through the windscreen of the car. It shows the light from the object reflected off the bonnet of the car and off the metal crash barrier at the side of the road. Experts say that this would be almost impossible to fake.

Satisfied that he was not dealing with a con man or a nutcase, Maussan visited Diaz at his home in Tepoztlan, Mexico, and tracked down a number of other witnesses who claimed to have seen the same type of UFO in the area at the time.

Maussan give Diaz a video camera and asked him to film the UFO when it next appeared. A few weeks later, Diaz awoke at 5 a.m., grabbed the camera and went outside and waited. Minutes later, the glowing spacecraft appeared, hovering about the house, and Diaz videoed it. Maussan was impressed, but he asked Diaz if he could get closer next time. Two months later, Diaz managed to video the craft hovering directly above him. Even more spectacular footage was to follow. On a third occasion, Diaz set the video camera up on a tripod in a field and locked it off. He filmed himself walking to the end of the field waving a torch. Suddenly the craft appeared directly above his head. It hovered there motionless for half-a-minute before disappearing. This is universally acknowledged as some of the best UFO footage ever shot.

Other UFOlogists have investigated the case and both German UFO author Michael Hesemann and alien abduction expert Dr John Mack have concluded that Diaz's story is credible.

'The Carlos Diaz case is the most important case of documented alien–human contact to have emerged in modern times,' says Hesemann, who first interviewed Diaz in 1994. 'Not only is he contacting these beings through encounters on the ships, but he also claims to be meeting these beings socially, since he believes some of them are living among us.'

Diaz says the beings are reluctant to fully disclose their origins. However, they did explain that they have been visiting Earth for thousands of years, and are particularly interested in our evolution which, compared to their own, has happened at a much faster rate. They are trying to learn why.

In his book *Passport to the Cosmos*, John Mack, Professor of Psychiatry at Harvard Medical School, says: 'Out of all the experiencers I have worked with, it is Carlos Diaz who seems to have developed the richest understanding of the interconnected web of nature. Diaz's experience of connecting with living creatures is so intense that he seems literally to become the thing he is describing.'

Diaz's experience, Mack claims, constitutes an 'awakening', a process that involves the evolution of consciousness. This is something that Mack regularly finds in abductees. A deep passion for ecological responsibility and an awareness of environmental matters are key to this spiritual transformation, Mack says. Indeed, Diaz told Mack that his contact with the aliens has given him a renewed ability to enjoy the beauties of the plant and a burning desire to protect the environment. This has become a driving force in his life and he makes passionate pleas for the environment at UFO conferences.

For Diaz's visiting extraterrestrials, these warnings come from the heart – if they have such an organ. Their civilisation was destroyed by an environmental catastrophe. If humankind carries on, on its current course, it is heading for total extinction, the aliens say. Because of his environmental predictions, Diaz has assumed the status of a visionary both in UFO circles and his hometown of Tepoztlan. But Diaz says he is no visionary, merely 'a messenger', and he has recently opened a UFO centre in Tepoztlan to inform visitors about UFOs and his experiences as a contactee.

Maussan thinks that Diaz's encounter and the new wave of Mexican sightings that began in 1991 might be connected to the Mayan prophecy found in the Dresden Codex. This says that the 'Fifth Sun', which began with the solar eclipse in 1991, would be heralded by catastrophic environmental changes.

Whatever the validity of Diaz's environmental message, few alien encounters come with photographic evidence that has stood up to such rigorous scrutiny.

Global Encounters

Although sightings of UFOs are common, contact with aliens is still comparatively rare. But on 15 September 1994, two close encounters of the third kind occurred – on opposite sides of the globe.

The previous day, 14 September, the residents of the town of Ruwa in Zimbabwe had been treated to a massive pyrotechnic display in the sky over the northern part of South Africa. The celestial event was so powerful that, far to the north, MUFON co-ordinator for Africa Cynthia Hind heard a loud explosion that evening as she worked in her study in Zimbabwe's capital, Harare.

Soon after, Hind was swamped with reports of unusual aerial activity. A Russian satellite launch had taken place that day, and many of sightings, she discovered, were due to the ejected

Long- haired alien by Oriana Fenwick.

nose cone, which had re-entered the atmosphere over Africa. However, other reports, describing 'a brilliant cigar-shaped light moving at tree top level and changing direction,' could not be explained so easily.

This is what a group of young children from the Ariel Primary School in Ruwa saw the following day, 15 September. They spotted a cigar-shaped object hanging low in the sky. Suddenly

Craft and black alien by Brian Robins

the object disappeared. The children were puzzled, but soon forgot about what they had seen. But they were to receive an incredible reminder on the morning of 16 September.

At 10 a.m., it was break time and the children rushed out of their classrooms into the playground. That morning they would be unsupervised. The school's headmaster, Colin Mackie, and the thirteen teachers stayed inside for a staff meeting. Suddenly, there was a purple light flashing in the sky. Moments later, a large disc-shaped UFO appeared and began slowly descending into an empty field next to the school.

When the children were interviewed by Cynthia Hind several days after the event, their descriptions of the craft varied widely. Some were sure that there was only one craft. Others saw one main craft with three smaller ones. Eleven-year-old Guy had described it as 'multi-coloured with black, green and silver stripes', while ten-year-old Fifi said it had a 'golden glow that was so bright it was difficult to see'.

The German UFO researcher Michael Hesemann interviewed forty-four of the children in 1997 and believes that the discrepancies do not mean that the children were making it up.

'Given the number of witnesses and the shock of the event, you would expect the descriptions to vary,' he says.

Piecing together the consistent parts of the witness reports, investigators concluded that what had landed in the field was a large glowing disc, with a flattened dome on top. It was surrounded by yellow lights or portholes and extended a three-legged landing gear.

As the craft landed, balls of light, or perhaps miniature discs, appeared and flew around for a short while. Some children began screaming and ran back to the school building; others stood their ground, transfixed. In all, some one hundred children witnessed the landing. Some of the braver children even edged forward. They stood on logs to get a better view of the craft, which was about 220 yards away.

To the children's amazement, three beings emerged. They were humanoid and wore shiny, black, tight-fitting, one-piece suits. One remained near the craft, while the other two approached the children. They moved in what the children described as a 'slow-motion wobble'. Those closest said the aliens were about four feet tall. One had long black hair; the other two were bald. Their faces were dark and they had small noses and mouths. And some of the children said they had metal bands around their heads.

But the key feature that struck the children was the creatures' large black eyes. They said, they looked like 'cat's eyes' and several of the children said they received 'messages' after looking into the creatures' eyes. This method of communication is frequently reported by abductees. Abduction investigator Dr David Jacobs says that aliens use their eyes to implant ideas in the minds of humans. And looking deep into a human's eyes also allows the aliens to perform what one alien abductee called a 'mindscan'.

'When I looked into their eyes it is like they can see into my soul,' she told Dr Jacobs.

In Ruwa, Hesemann believes that the aliens used this procedure to implant an important ecological message. He says: 'The children who were not afraid and who managed to stare directly into the eyes of the beings began to hear a voice inside their head. Instantly, they got the thought that the ETs had come because humans were destroying the planet and that the children should participate in an effort to stop this.'

One of the children, eleven-year-old Carry Evans, said: 'I was afraid they wanted to attack us because we did something wrong, or destroyed something precious to them. I believe that the aliens came to warn us because the Earth is going to be destroyed by us.'

Headmaster Colin Mackie said that whatever the aliens had done seemed to work. All the children who reported receiving the telepathic communication from the extraterrestrials later became actively involved in ecological projects.

Once the beings had imparted their message, they went back to their ship, which began to flash. Then it was gone in a burst of light. The entire encounter had lasted about three minutes.

Several of the children who ran back to the school tried to inform the teachers, but they were still in the staff meeting. The only adult nearby was Alyson Kirkman, who was on duty at the tuck shop.

'Come quickly and see, ' begged one of the children. 'There's a little man running around in a one-piece suit with a band around his head.'

She laughed and said: 'Pull the other one.'

By the time the staff meeting was over, the alien ship had disappeared. At first, none of the teachers believed what the children were telling them. Some were hysterical. All of them had plainly been affected by some extraordinary event and it slowly began to dawn on the staff that the children's fantastic stories might be true. It was then that the UFO investigators were called in.

Whatever happened at the Ariel School that day, the events certainly had a profound impact on the children, especially those who claimed to have interacted with the 'alien' beings. The Ruwa children were left deeply changed by their experience.

Several thousand miles away in Mexico, it was still 15 September 1994. Between 8 p.m. that evening and 1 a.m. the following morning, air traffic controllers in Mexico reported UFO activity over the town of Metapec to the west of Mexico City. Soon, reports began rolling in that hundreds of people had seen a UFO hovering over the rooftops.

Among the witnesses were two sisters, Sara and Erika Cuevas. They had been driving back to their home in Metapec at the time of the sightings. As they approached the town, they saw a reddish disc in the sky, which they estimated to be about seventy feet in diameter. Eager to make a record of the event, when they arrived home, Sara rushed inside to get her video camera, but she soon discovered that the camera was not working, and nor were any of the electrical appliances in their home.

The two sisters went up to the roof for a better view of the UFO, which was still in plain sight in the sky. As they stood watching, two smaller red objects shot out of it and descended into the field next to their house. Two hours later, this extraordinary display was repeated. This time seven smaller discs ended up darting around on the ground. As they moved about in the field, they flattened the stalks of maize – without any physical contact, witnesses said – forming a large geometric pattern. Sudden, one of the discs exploded. Hundreds of tiny balls, resembling 'eyes', appeared, said one witness. This caused alarm and panic among the spectators.

The next day, UFO investigator and TV journalist Jaime Maussan, along with dozens of other reporters, arrived to interview witnesses. The investigators also charted a helicopter to film the strange pattern in the field. Despite this media circus and the numerous witnesses around the town, Sara Cuevas' husband refused to believe her when she told him what she had seen. Annoyed by his scepticism, she vowed to stay up all night, video camera in hand, in case the UFO returned.

Her sister Erika volunteered to wait with her, but they were to be disappointed. There was no sign of the craft. However, in the middle of the night, the sisters saw a mysterious glow in the field. There appeared to be a light about thirty yards away, but when they moved to get a better view, they realised that it was not a light at all it was a glowing figure who was standing in the middle of the crop pattern that had appeared the previous night.

Sara lifted her video camera and pressed record. This time the machine worked. She recorded three minutes of videotape, showing the figure standing still, shrouded in brilliant luminescence. On the soundtrack you can hear the reaction of the sisters. Sara says: 'What is it? That's horrible. Oh my God… Erika, it's so ugly.'

Then, suddenly the creature simply vanished.

A computer analysis of the Cuevas sisters' video was performed by Professor Victor Quesada at the University of Mexico's Polytechnical Institute. He estimated that the figure was about four feet three inches tall and some twenty-five yards from the camera. From its shape, he concluded that it was not human. According to Quesada, the light came from the creature itself. It was too bright and too evenly illuminated to be a mannequin. Computer enhancements revealed a large, terrifying insect-like head with a small stalk-like proboscis or antenna. And a similar enhancement of the lower part of the body revealed it was carrying some kind of instrument in its hand.

Jaime Maussan and another Mexican UFO researcher, Mario Torres, made an analysis of the soil and plants in the field. Anomalies were found in both. The temperature of the soil was found to be much higher than the surrounding ground. Radiation levels were 350 per cent above the background and strange cellular changes had occurred in the leaves of the pumpkin plants there. Unfortunately, investigators at Metapec discovered nothing else to shed any light on what the sisters caught on video that night.

The children in Zimbabwe did not have access to a video camera, so the two cases could not be compared. The best they could do was some interesting drawings of the benign creatures they had met. Interestingly, there is a correlation between the heavenly gods in Aztec myth and the myths of Zimbabwe. When Dr John Mack began investigating the Ruwa case in 1994, he asked the advice of an African *sangoma*, or medicine man, named Credo Mutwa, whose knowledge of African myth is renowned throughout the continent. Mutwa explained that for thousands of years, local people had spoken of 'star people' who came to Earth in 'magic sky boats'. The creatures, with large, black, 'cat-like' eyes are what the Zulu called *mantindane*. The Australian aborigines called them *wandinja* and often depicted them in rock paintings. In Zulu culture, the *mantindane* are the bringers of knowledge – Quetzalcoatl – though they also spread disease and confusion among humankind. But Mutwa says that they are not extraterrestrials at all. They are the future descendants of humankind coming back in time.

But what was the significance of the encounters in Zimbabwe and Mexico occurring at the same time? UFOlogists speculated that it might be part of an increasingly intrusive pattern of alien visitations.

Monster on the Moor

In 1987 ex-police officer Philip Spencer made contact in the unlikely setting of Ilkley Moor in Yorkshire. On 1 December, he left his home in the town of Ilkley at around 7:15 a.m. He was planning to visit his father-in-law in the village of East Morton on the far side of the moor. History does not record whether he was wearing a hat, but he did take with him a compass, for navigation, and a camera with which he hoped to photograph some panoramic views from the moor tops.

It was a still, winter's day. The moor was empty and peaceful that morning, but he was conscious of a mysterious humming sound as he climbed a hill towards a group of trees. Ignoring it, he continued on his way. As the path he was following skirted an old quarry, his attention was attracted by something moving below him. Further along the path he came upon a small green creature standing just ten feet away. It was not like anything he had seen before. Apart from being green, it was short and hunched over, with massively long arms. It waved dismissively at him with one of them, before scuttling off.

Although he was dumbstruck, Spencer had the presence of mind to fumble for his camera and photograph the creature before it disappeared behind an outcrop. Then he pursued it, only to be confronted by a silver disc-shaped flying saucer hovering in front of him before soaring away into the sky and disappearing into the clouds.

Dazed and bewildered, Spencer decided to head back to Ilkley. On the way he noticed that the compass he was carrying had been affected by the encounter. The needle now pointed south instead of north. From the distance he had travelled, Spencer reckoned that he had been away from home for no more than an hour. It should have been no later than 8.15 a.m. when he got back to Ilkley. To his surprise, the streets were already bustling with shoppers and the church clock said it was 10 a.m. There was an hour and forty-five minutes he could not account for.

He began to wonder if the encounter had been a bizarre dream. But there was one way he could find out. He jumped on the next bus into Keithley, where there was a shop with a one-hour film processing service. Within an hour, he had confirmation. Exposure number ten showed a clear image of a small green alien being.

When he eventually returned home, Spencer showed the picture to his wife. She did not know what to make of it. But Spencer could not leave it there. He needed to contact someone with expert knowledge. As an ex-policeman he was concerned about his reputation. So using a Post Office box number to protect his identity, he wrote to top British UFOlogist Jenny Randles.

Randles was sceptical of his account but forwarded Spencer's letter to fellow UFOlogist Peter Hough. He too was unconvinced. After some discussion, both eventually agreed that they should pursue the matter. While Randles and Hough were dithering, Spencer had found the number of paranormal investigator Arthur Tomlinson listed in a directory in Ilkley library. Tomlinson interviewed Spencer and then, seeking a second opinion, sent an account of the meeting to Hough. Hough instantly recognised the case, and the two of them decided to collaborate.

On 3 January 1988, Hough went to see Spencer and accused him of making the whole thing up. 'What would you say to someone who said: "Come on, you've built a dummy, taken it up on the moor and photographed it?"' he asked.

Perhaps because of his police training, Spencer was not fazed by this line of questioning.

'I'm not particularly interested in what other people think,' he replied. 'I know what I saw, and if people don't believe me, that's up to them. I've got nothing to gain by doing that. I don't see the sense, I've got better things to do with my time.'

Impressed by Spencer's sincerity, Hough began conducting a thorough scientific investigation of this story. An examination of the place where the encounter occurred turned up nothing. The levels of radiation in the area were normal. There were no magnetic anomalies there either. So what could have affected Spencer's compass?

Hough turned to Dr Ed Spooner, head of the Department of Electrical Engineering and Electronics at the University of Manchester Institute of Science and Technology (UMIST). He carried out some tests on a compass identical to Spencer's and found that strong magnets had no permanent effect on the needle. However, a pulsed field, or one switched on and off again rapidly, did. This effect could be produced using mains electricity or even a car battery. But it was a dangerous procedure and required specialist knowledge. In 1990 powerful industrial magnets from Japan were found to cause the same effect, but they were not available in 1987 when the polarity of Spencer's compass was reversed.

Hough's investigation then focused on the 35mm camera that Spencer had used. It had a light meter, but it had been broken for several years. It would have been hard to produce a convincing fake with such an inadequate piece of equipment. Nevertheless, Hough sent the negative of Spencer's alien image to Kodak photographic expert Peter Sutherst, who said that the film had not been tampered with. However, he reported: 'It is underexposed by at least two stops. It is usual for these films to produce grainy pictures when underexposed. The negative shows a degree of camera shake, making it difficult to decide what the small figure might be. Identification is made even more of a problem because of underexposure.'

This underexposure raised doubts. It was hazy that morning and Spencer had set the shutter speed at around 1/60th of a second and opened the lens to its widest aperture. The camera had also been loaded with 400 ASA film, which should have been almost impossible to underexpose. Others point out that the sky is too bright. It would have taken around half-an-hour to reach the place where the encounter had taken place. That would have made it around 7:45 a.m. Dawn didn't break until a couple of minutes before 8:00 a.m. that winter morning in West Yorkshire.

Hough looked into the possibility of computer enhancement of the image. But Sutherst pointed out that image enhancement was a costly exercise. He doubted its benefits in this case. 'The size, distance of the subject, camera movement and underexposure mean that there is insufficient detail available to enhance,' he said. Since then attempts to enhance the image in Britain, the US and Japan have all failed.

The only other place to look for clues was in Spencer's mind. Spencer was troubled by the missing time he had experienced and Hough arranged a meeting with clinical psychologist Jim Singleton, who practised regressional hypnosis. This is a technique used to recover lost memories.

Under hypnosis, Spencer relived his conscious memory of walking up the path towards the trees. But then a new chunk of memory emerged. The transcript of the session read: 'I'm walking along the moor. Oh! It's quite windy. There's a lot of clouds. Walking up towards the trees, I see this little something, can't tell, but he's green. It's moving towards me. Oh! I can't move. I'm stuck. He's still coming towards me. And I still can't move... I'm stuck, and everything's gone fuzzy. I'm... I'm floating along in the air... I want to get down! And this green thing's walking ahead of me, and I don't like it.'

Apparently, as Spencer drew level with the trees, he stopped, aware through the early morning haze that something was coming down the hill towards him. He froze as a green being with large eyes and pointed ears approached. Then he said: 'I still can't move. I'm going around the corner and this green thing's in front of me. Oh, God, I want to get down. There's a.... there's a big silver saucer thing, and there's a door in it, and I don't want to go in there! Everything's gone black now...'

Spencer wanted to escape, but found he was paralysed. The alien started walking back up the hill. Spencer found himself levitated, helplessly following the creature. It was then, in the quarry, that he first saw a silver disc. There was a door in the disc, then darkness enveloped him. He awoke to find himself in a small room illuminated by a bright light. A voice in his head told him not to be afraid. He was put on a table and a beam of light scanned the contours of his body. There were a number of creatures in the room.

'The creatures seemed part of a team,' he said. 'They weren't acting as individuals, but more like bees, as if they were doing what they were programmed to do.'

Spencer also gave a detailed description of one of them: 'He's quite small, about four foot. He's got a nose and only has a little mouth. His hands are enormous. He's got three big fingers, like big sausages and his arms were long. He's got funny feet – they're like a V-shape, like two big toes.'

Although Spencer referred to the alien as 'he', he gave no reason for deciding that the alien was male. He gave no information about primary or secondary sexual characteristics. But one thing that struck Hough was that the aliens Spencer had seen had cloven hooves.

Spencer then felt a strange sensation up his nose and he was accompanied out of the room by one of the several creatures present. In the corridor, Spencer looked out through a window to see the Earth below. It was only then that he realised he was in outer space. A door opened in the wall of the corridor, and he was led out onto a gantry that ran around the walls of a large room. In the middle of the room, there was a spinning ball. His camera and the compass that were hanging by cords around his neck were drawn towards the ball as if my magnetism.

In another room, he was shown a film depicting a polluted Earth where billions were starving. After that he was engulfed by blackness again. He had no further memories until he found himself back on the moor with no recollection of the abduction. What Hough and Singleton found particularly impressive was that, even under hypnosis, he expressed surprise at seeing the creature and taking its picture.

An examination of the historical records also proved fruitful. It seems that 1987 was not the first time that little green men had paid a visit to the area. In 1851 one famous incident had taken place at White Wells, just three hundred yards from where Spencer's encounter had taken place. The health spa there is built around a natural spring. One morning the caretaker, William Butterfield, arrived to open up, only to find that his key spun around in the lock by itself. Inside he found a bath full of aliens.

'All around the spring, dipping into it, were a lot of little creatures dressed in green, none more than eighteen inches, making chatter and jabber,' Butterfield said. 'They seemed to be taking a bath with their clothes on. Soon, however, one or two of them began to make off, bounding over the walls like squirrels. Then the whole tribe went, helter skelter, toppling and tumbling, head over heels.'

Butterfield ran after them. They disappeared up the path that

Philip Spencer followed 172 years later.

No satisfactory explanation has been given of what happened on Ilkley Moor that day – any more than there is of the day Philip Spencer walked up that path. Although doubts have been raised about the photograph, it has resisted all attempts to expose it as a fake. As Spencer says himself, he had nothing to gain from carrying out a hoax. He is certainly not seeking publicity or even attention. Throughout, he has insisted on using the name 'Philip Spencer', which is a pseudonym. He is not after money either and has turned down several lucrative offers from newspapers and television companies to go public. He has never sought to capitalise on his encounter and has insisted that his real identity be protected throughout. Otherwise, he says, 'it would ruin me both socially and professionally.'

Israeli Encounters

A wave of alien encounters that has taken place in modern Israel also have ancient resonances. In biblical times, beings fell from the heavens and later became the mortal enemies of the Hebrew nations. They were called *nefilim*, which means the 'fallen ones', and the giants that appear in the Bible were their descendants. Since the late 1980s, these giants have returned to Israel. And they are not shy about their presence. They have allowed their craft to be filmed. They chose to contact unimpeachable witnesses and have left abundant physical evidence.

Israel's new UFO age began on the evening of 28 September 1987, when twenty-seven-year-old auto mechanic Ami Achrai was driving down a road near the sea just south of Haifa. He saw what he took to be a helicopter hovering just above the sands of Shikmona Beach. It appeared to be in difficulties. He stopped his car for a better look. It was then he realised that the hovering craft was no helicopter. It was a disc-shaped flying saucer which gave off a bright red flash, then disappeared.

Achrai reported the sighting to the police, who referred him to UFOlogist Hadassah Arbel. Two days later, they returned to the site and discovered striking evidence that a UFO had been there. It seems the blinding red flash emitted by the craft had burned a fifty-foot ellipse in the sands of the beach. And the image of the space-craft's pilot at his controls was imprinted in nearby vegetation, which remained otherwise undamaged.

Seven years later, samples of the burnt sand were sent to the US television show *Sightings* by UFOlogist Barry Chamish. Under the heat of the studio lights, the burnt sand seemed to melt. The reason for this, a laboratory later discovered, was that the sand particles were coated in a hydrocarbon material with a low melting point. But the laboratory could offer no explanation as to why the sand was coated with this substance.

On 6 June 1988, the image of another ellipsoid craft was burned into the sands of Shikmona Beach, a few yards north of the first site. Then on 27 April 1989, two teenagers saw a UFO explode over Shikmona Beach. It disintegrated into thousands of shards that were strewn across the beach. When Israeli UFOlogists investigat-ed the sighting, they found fragments of a strange glowing white metal that was cool to the touch. The fragments even glowed under water. But when they were picked up, they turned into a white ash. Analysis revealed that they were made from a very pure form of magnesium. Scientists from the Technion Institute of Technology in Haifa also found that the levels of magnetism at the site were six thousand times higher that in the surrounding area.

The site itself has some biblical significance. About six hundred feet above Shikmona Beach is a shrine called Elijah's Cave. The prophet Elijah was said to have preached there. Inside there is the drawing of a saucer-shaped craft that bears a distinct resemblance to those seen over Shikmona Beach in modern times. Elijah has some other extraterrestrial connections. According to the Bible, in the nearby Carmel Mountains, Elijah challenged the Canaanites to a battle of Gods. Two bulls were tethered out in the open. Baal, the god of the Canaanites, was called upon to roast one of them, while Elijah called upon the Israelite god Yahweh to roast the other. The Canaanite god failed, but Elijah's god sent down a ray of light from the heavens that cooked the bull on the spot. Could this have been a death ray, and could a similar beam have been used to burn the sands of Shikmona Beach thousands of years later?

After the UFO exploded over Shikmona Beach, there was a lull in UFO sightings. But activity started again five years later. This time, it was focused on the small Israeli town of Kadima. On the morning of 20 April 1993, Tsiporet Carmel woke up to discover her house bathed in a strange glow. Outside she saw a strange craft on the ground. As she looked, it appeared to grow in size before her eyes. Some ten yards from the spacecraft, she saw the figure of a giant. It was about six feet seven inches and was clad in a one-piece metallic suit. On its head, it wore a helmet, which Tsiporet compared to a beekeeper's hat.

Unafraid, Tsiporet went outside and spoke to the creature.

'Why don't you take off your hat so I can see your face?' she said.

The creature's reply was delivered telepathically.

'That's the way it is,' it said.

The story of Tsiporet Carmel's encounter with the alien hit the newspapers. There had never been a publicised close encounter in Israel before and Tsiporet risked ridicule. Fortunately, the alien had left some physical evidence to back her story. A crop circle, some fifteen feet in diameter, was found where she had seen the alien spacecraft. Shards of a strange material were discovered inside the circle. On analysis this was found to be a very pure form of silicon. Ten days later, two more circles appeared just outside her back garden. They were soaked with a red liquid. The National Biological Laboratory in Ness Tziona analysed the liquid and found that it was composed mostly of cadmium. It was also found in other crop circles subsequently discovered in the area.

Two other residents of Kadima reported similar encounters. In May, the town treasurer, Shosh Vahud, claimed to have met a giant alien, which visited her bedroom. She woke to see a six feet seven inch, round-faced creature in a silver jump-suit circling her bed, as if 'floating on his shoes'. Telepathically it assured her that it meant her no harm and she relaxed. After a few minutes, the creature floated out through the wall. Shosh dismissed the encounter as a dream until she spotted a fifteen-foot crop circle outside her win-

dow the next morning. UFOlogists found both cadmium and silicon within the circle.

In June, the giant alien turned its attention to the village of
Burgata, about three miles away. Hannah Somech was working in
her kitchen one day when she saw her dog go flying across the
room and crash into a wall. Outside she saw a six feet seven inch
being clad in metallic overalls examining her pickup truck.

Like Tsiporet, Hanna was a tough Israeli woman. She marched
right up to the alien.

'What did you do to my dog?' she demanded.

Again the reply came telepathically.

'Go away,' the creature said. 'I'm busy. I could crush you like an
ant if I wanted to.'

Again, after the incident, a fifteen-foot circle was found in
Hannah's back garden. The grass in the circle was soaked with the
same red cadmium liquid as in Kadima.

In December 1994 the village of Yatzitz, twelve miles east of
Rishon Letzion, played host to another giant. Herzl Casatini, the
village security chief, was visiting his friend Danny Ezra when
they heard a massive explosion. Ezra's house shook to its founda-
tions. Herzl rushed to the door to find out what was happening. But
when he opened the door, he found himself face to face with a
giant, again clad in a metallic one-piece. This one was over eight
feet tall and its face was obscured by a strange 'haze'. Discretion
being the better part of valour, Herzl slammed the door in its face
and called the cops.

When the police arrived, they found boot tracks. Some of the
tracks had sunk in over a foot in the hard mud. This meant whatever had made them must have weighed over a ton. The creature
seemed to 'walk' on its toes, as the heel was rarely indented more
than two inches. Always on the alert for terrorist activity, the Israeli
army arrived on the scene. The military trackers were equally puzzled. They followed the tracks for over five miles. In some places
the distance between boot prints was over ten feet. They could only
speculate that the tracks had been left by an unknown cult. But
UFOlogists made the connection between the tall aliens the various

witness had seen and the giants of ancient times. According to the Bible, King Og of Bashan had to have a bed that was thirteen feet long. Bashan's kingdom included the Golan Heights, home to a mysterious monument called the Gilgal Refaim, or 'circle of the giants'. It consists of five concentric rings of stone – the outermost is 522 feet in diameter. Like other such monuments it has celestial connections. Openings align with the solstices and the rising of Sirius in 3000 BCE. Otherwise archaeologists are puzzled. It pre-dates the pyramids by five hundred years and no other structure in the Middle East remotely resembles it. The indigenous people of the area at that time were nomads who did not involve themselves in building megaliths. However, according to the Bible, a bunch of outsiders did visit the Golan Heights back then. And they were giants.

After Yatzitz, the modern-day giants spread out, visiting many other Israeli towns. Then in 1995, they returned to Kadima, with horrifying results. One morning in January, Amos and Rachel Gueta woke to find their livestock killed and mutilated. Sheep, chickens and even their farm dog were found dead. The heads of the sheep had been shaved and there were holes in the skulls that appeared to have been made by a drill. No satisfactory explanation has ever been offered.

In 1996 over a dozen UFOs were filmed over Israel. In August one flying saucer with distinctive square vents was filmed on three successive nights, hovering over the Israeli town of Hatzar. And Yugoslav immigrant Spasso Maximovitch managed to film two UFOs colliding over Rosh Haayin. MUFON's Jeff Sainio has examined the film and declared it genuine.

'The acceleration, light, size, and explosion are not explainable in any conventional way that I know of,' he says. 'This case remains unidentified.'

The following November, what looked like a 'flying brain' was filmed hovering over Tel Aviv. No one has yet been able to explain what it was.

Giants are not the only aliens to visit Israel. In December 1996, a Netanya household reported regular contact with small 'Greys' –

the first time this species of alien had been seen in the Middle East. Physical evidence was produced to support this story, including stones that can melt ice although they have no known energy source.

It is noticeable that the giants were very selective about who they visited. All the contactees were women. They were all middle-class – making them, in the eyes of the authorities, credible witnesses – and they were all in their late thirties. When Tsiporet Carmel and Shosh Vahud appeared on TV, Clara Kahonov from Holon, south of Tel Aviv, came forward saying that she, too, had been visited by a giant. In Rishon Letzion, just twelve miles from Holon, Baya Shimon claimed that she had seen more than one. In early July 1993, two huge, bald beings beamed themselves into her seventh-floor apartment. As they floated around her apartment, they told her, telepathically, not to be afraid. They spent a few minutes dusting her shelves with a foul-smelling yellow powder, then disappeared the way they had come. At 3 a.m. the following night, a dozen of then turned up the same way.

Seven of the cases have been particularly well documented. In two cases, the contactees reported unexpected pregnancies. Three contactees have been haunted telepathically since. Although none of the women knew each other, they all reported seeing the same thing. Each independently described meeting six feet seven inch, round-faced giants. And in each case, the visitor left physical evidence of its presence. It seems that giants are roaming Israel today, just as they did thousands of years ago.

2 Abducted

First Contact

From the first sighting of flying saucers in 1947, there was a puzzle. What were the aliens doing here and why did they not make contact directly? It was only when UFOlogists began investigating the phenomenon of alien abduction that it became all to frighteningly clear what they were doing here and, it seemed, in their own sinister way they had been contacting us all along.

The first well-documented alien abduction took place on the night of 19 September 1961. Forty-one-year-old child-welfare worker Betty Hill and her thirty-nine-year-old mailman husband Barney were returning home to

Betty and Barney Hill, abducted on board a UFO, September 1961.

Portsmouth, New Hampshire, after a vacation in southern Canada. Having crossed back into the US near Colebrook, New Hampshire, at around 10 p.m., they took Interstate Route 3, which winds through the mountains to the east of the state. Out on the dark, lonely road, the Hills were puzzled by a strange, large 'white star' that seemed to be following them. Barney told his wife that it was probably a plane heading for Montreal.

There was little traffic on the highway and the Hills decided to stop to let their dog Delsey out of the car for some exercise. While Betty walked the dog, Barney got out his binoculars to take a closer look at the strange light. When Betty and Delsey came back to the car, they drove off again. But a few minutes later, Barney felt an urgent and irrational need to stop the car and get out. By now they were at an isolated spot called Indian Head. Barney seemed completely hypnotised by the light in the sky. He ignored Betty's pleading to get back into the car and walked off in the direction of the light, disappearing into the undergrowth at the side of the road.

Studying the strange light through his binoculars, it became clear to Barney that they were being followed by a strange craft. It was banana shaped, with pointed tips and windows. Through large windows, Barney could see figures.

'I don't believe this!' he yelled as his yanked the binoculars from his eyes. 'They're going to capture us!'

In panic, he fled back to the car and they sped off southwards. The panic did not last. Instead, a strange feeling of detachment seemed to come over them. This is a phenomenon know to UFOlogists as the 'Oz Factor', which often accompanies encounters. The Hills remember an electronic beeping sound, followed by a bump. In no time at all they found themselves just seventeen miles from Portsmouth. The UFO had disappeared and the couple drove home without further incident.

The following day, the Hills noticed some peculiar blotches on the car. The paint had been removed to show the bare metal underneath. Betty's sister took a look. She had seen a UFO herself four years before, and had taken an interest in the subject. The patches, she suggested, might be magnetised. She had heard that UFOs generated massive magnetic fields that could stall car engines. Barney was sceptical but the Hills checked it out and they found that, when

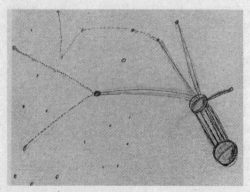

Star map drawn by Betty Hill during her UFO abduction in 1961.

they passed a compass over the bodywork, the needle swung wildly over the blotched areas.

Realising that their encounter had been closer than they thought, the Hills called nearby Pease Air Force Base to report their UFO sighting. They were told nothing at the time but records released since under the Freedom of Information Act show that there had been UFO activity in the area at the time. At 2:15 a.m. on the morning of 20 September, a UFO flying in the vicinity of White Mountains had been tracked on military radar.

Even though the Hills had no idea that the military had also seen the UFO, they decided to write to a national UFO group and on 21 October 1961, astronomer and UFOlogist Walter Webb visited the Hills in their home.

During the interview Barney revealed other worrying details he had noticed after the encounter. His shoes were scuffed as if he had been dragged along the ground and he had a pain in his back that he could not account for.

Betty had also been badly affected by the incident. On 30 September, she began a series of disturbing nightmares. For several nights, she dreamed of strange creatures with horrible faces and cat-like eyes who were out to kidnap her and her husband.

One peculiar fact emerged from their account. They had no recollection of the thirty-five miles from Indian Head to the point where they were just seventeen miles from Portsmouth. Both their watches had stopped and when they got home it was much later than they thought. Two hours seemed to have gone missing. Both the 'interrupted journey' and 'missing time' are now recognised as classic features of alien abductions.

With no logical explanation of what had happened to them that night, the Hills began to fret. Betty was tormented by her dreams and Barney was becoming paranoid. The following spring things got so bad that they sought medical advice. Their doctor referred them to a number of specialists who were of little help. Eventually they found themselves in the Boston office of psychiatrist Dr Benjamin Simon, a Harvard-trained expert in stress management.

Dr Simon listened to their UFO story and Betty told him about

Two sketches by Barney Hill (the right under hypnosis) of the UFO entity leader.

her dreams. A medical man, he tended to reject the idea of a paranormal explanation. Nevertheless he recognised that something to do with their fateful journey was disturbing the Hills and he recommended regressional hypnosis to get to the bottom of it.

Betty and Barney were regressed separately, but a number of images that surfaced from their unconscious memories were strikingly similar. Reliving the experience caused considerable stress and they sometimes reacted with terror. On more than one occasion Dr Simon had to get staff to help him hold down Barney while he relived the events of that night and fought to escape from the ghouls that were plaguing him.

After six months of hypnosis, Dr Simon was coming to realise that he had a unique case on his hands. No matter what he did he

UFOs: Artist's impression of the UFO encounter of Betty and Barney Hill in the White Mountains of New Hampshire, 1961.

could not shake the Hills' story. They were not making up what they saw and they could not be sharing a single delusion. Their stories dovetailed together so perfectly that he could come to only one conclusion – what they were telling him was real.

According to the story they revealed under hypnotic regression, the light that they had seen in the sky was indeed a UFO. It had landed beside the road and somehow rendered the Hills semi-conscious. The couple were then forcibly taken on board the spacecraft by small beings with whitish skins and large cat-like eyes, like the ones Betty had seen in her nightmares. These are the 'Greys' that are now so frequently reported in abductions.

Once on board, the couple were separated. A voice in their heads told them not to be afraid and they were given medical examinations. Betty had a long needle inserted into her abdomen. This, she was told telepathically, was a type of pregnancy test. Meanwhile Barney had his penis inserted in some sort of suction device and semen was extracted. The alien's inordinate interest in our genetic make up became another standard feature of abductions.

Other samples were taken from the Hills during their abduction – notably clippings of their nails and hair. New to the Earth, apparently the aliens were particularly bemused by the differences in the couple's skin colour. Betty was white; Barney, who was Ethiopian by birth, was black.

After these tests, the aliens showed Betty around the UFO. At one point, she was shown a 'star map' which, she was told, showed all the star systems that the aliens had visited on their travels. Some stars systems were joined by solid lines. These indicated regular trading routes. Other were joined by dotted lines, indicating the routes of occasional expeditions.

Under hypnosis, Betty made a sketch of her recollection of the map. It was sent to astronomer Majorie Fish. She plotted the location of all the stars systems within fifty light-years of Earth that were likely to contain habitable planets. It matched. From this, Fish was able to work out that the alien's home planet orbited the star Zeta Reticulli.

Before Betty left the spacecraft, she asked her alien captors for a memento to prove that she and Barney had really been on board. The aliens' leader agreed, and Betty chose a large book which contain tightly packed columns of characters that she likened to hieroglyphics. But just as the couple were about to leave the ship, the alien who had said that Betty could take the book changed his mind. Betty said it appeared as if his decision had been overruled by the other aliens. Despite her protests, Betty had to leave without it. Eventually the Hills were led back outside and lost consciousness. They woke up again inside the car, some distance from the site of the abduction, and the UFO was gone.

Under hypnosis, Barney sketched the alien craft, while Betty's description of the aliens themselves was drawn by local artist Dave Barker. The drawing he produced shows what we now know as the classic 'Grey'.

Betty and Barney Hill's abduction has become a landmark in UFO history. Boston journalist John Fuller wrote the Hill's story up as *The Interrupted Journey,* which was serialised around the world. It was later made into the 1975 TV movie called *The UFO Incident*. It is a key case in UFOlogy and established the use of regressional hypnosis in the field. The case also fired the public's imagination, and the threat of alien abduction suddenly gained credibility.

However, Betty Hill is sceptical about many of the abduction claims that have been made since she and Barney were taken.

'Real abductions are rare and they are all different,' she says. 'Ours did not involve anything sexual. And today almost all investigators are using suggestive hypnosis rather than the medical hypnosis Dr Simon used with Barney and me.'

Betty believes that she and Barney were abducted because of their behaviour – 'stopping the car, looking though binoculars, waving and shouting. We were showing curiosity, and maybe this made them curious of us,' she said.

At the time, the couple found that their alien abduction story was widely accepted. But since then, Betty feels, all the talk of a sexual motive for the abductions – 'weird fantasies,' she says – has turned the public off. However, she also thinks that the US government knows a great deal more about UFOs than it is letting on.

'What little they release is done to test the public's reaction,' she says.

Lurid Tale

One of the most lurid abductions occurred before the Hills' abduction case hit the headlines. It happened to a young Brazilian farmer named Antonio Villas-Boas, but the sexual nature of the story meant that it could not be published in the 1950s.

On 5 October 1957, Villas-Boas was in his room after a party. When he look out of his window, he saw a bright fluorescent light hovering just above the tree line of a nearby wood. He called his brother Jaoa who also witnessed the sighting. Neither of the men could explain what they saw and the object soon disappeared.

Antonio Villas Boas, being medically examined following his abduction by UFO in Brazil, on 15 October 1957.

Then on the night of 16 October 1957, Villas-Boas was working late in his field when he observed a strange circular object coming towards him. He tried to drive away in his tractor but the engine cut out and lights went out. He was paralysed as the object started to land just a few feet away from him.

As the UFO approached the ground, it deployed three telescopic legs, which it settled on. He was still recoiling in shock when he felt several hands grabbing him. He shouted for help but no one came and, before he knew what was happening, he was being led inside the space ship.

Inside he was taken into a large, brightly lit room, which had a metal pole running from the floor to the ceiling. The creatures talked among themselves in a strange growling language. They stripped him naked and anointed him with some strange oily fluid. Then he was left alone in the room.

Villas-Boas found himself becoming very tired and he lay down on what he took to be a couch. Soon after that the door opened and a naked woman came in. She was more beautiful than any woman he had ever seen before and was indistinguishable from a human female, except for her bright red pubic hair. Without a word, the creature indicated that she wanted to have sexual intercourse with him. He obliged. After he had ejaculated the woman got up to go. But before she left the room, she pointed to her stomach and then to the sky. He took this to mean that she was going to have his baby somewhere out in outer space.

He was then given a brief tour of the ship. The aliens did not talk to him but, rudely, continued to talk among themselves. During the tour, he tried to steal a piece of alien hardware as proof of this abduction and he managed to grab a 'clock-like instrument'. He had almost smuggled it off the ship with him but a keen-eyed alien spotted it and took it from him. Then the aliens pushed Villas-Boas unceremoniously out of the craft into a field. The ship took off and soared away into the sky at a tremendous speed.

It was several weeks before he told his mother and brother what had happened and it was a further two years before he sought professional help. He was later interviewed by many UFO researchers, the first of which was Dr Olavo Fontes, Brazilian representative of the Aerial Phenomena Research Organisation.

Every investigator who has interviewed Villas-Boas subsequently has been impressed with him as a witness. His story never changed and when he cannot answer a question he never tries to embellish. He was seen as a man of low intelligence but his story is too full of detail and strangeness to be made up by such a simple person. He is regarded as genuine and has never made any money from his experience.

The Voice of God

Following the airing of *The UFO Incident*, telling the Hills' story, there was a sudden surge in the reporting of alien abductions. Jumping on the bandwagon, the *National Enquirer* offered $1 million for definitive proof of extraterrestrial life and up to $10,000 for

Betty Andreasson-Luca, 1990.

the best UFO story. One of the stories that was sent in came from Betty Andreasson of Ashburnham, Massachusetts.

On the night of 25 January 1967, Betty was deeply perplexed. Her husband had been involved in a major car accident and was in hospital seriously ill. A devout Christian, Betty Andreasson was at home, praying hard for his recovery.

At around 7 p.m., she thought that her prayers had been answered. The family home was plunged into darkness, and a diffuse pink light shone in through the kitchen window. But when Betty's father looked outside, he saw what looked more like emissaries of the devil. In the yard was a group of small creatures that looked like 'Halloween freaks'. One of them turned to meet his gaze. The creature's eyes made him feel 'kinda queer' and he blacked out.

When the lights in the house came back on, Betty Andreasson saw her parents and her seven children standing their motionless, as if frozen. She, too, was rooted to the floor in terror. Four creatures, wreathed in haze, entered the house through the back door, which was locked. They were about four feet tall and were dressed in skin-tight blue uniforms. The heads were bulbous with almond-shaped eyes. When the family finally snapped out of their trance, they discovered that they had been unconscious for about three hours and forty minutes. Only Betty and her father had any recollection of anything at all that had happened. Even their memories were dim. It was only ten years later, when Andreasson was undergoing a session of regressional hypnosis that, the full story came out.

Based on what she had learned under hypnosis, Betty Andreasson wrote up the story and sent it to the *National Enquirer*. Although it would later be seen as one of the greatest UFO abduction stories on record, the *Enquirer* did not follow it up.

Undeterred by the *Enquirer's* rebuff, Betty Andreasson later responded to a newspaper article written by the scientist Dr J. Allen Hynek, founder of the Center for UFO Studies. In the article, he had appealed for contactees. There was a huge response right across the US and it was many months before investigator Jules Vailancourt turned up in Ashburnham. He was immediately interested in the case as there was a corroborating witness – Betty's father. Vailancourt decided that it merited further investigation and called in a regressional hypnosis expert, Henry J. Edelson. In fourteen sessions with Edelson between April and July 1977, Andreasson's amazing story unfolded.

It seems that, once the aliens had entered her home, the rest of her family were put into a deep trance. Only Betty remained conscious. The tallest alien, who called himself 'Quazgaa', asked her to accompany them. Andreasson was told that they had come to help the human race, which was in danger of destroying itself – the same message that contactees had been given before. It is not clear whether Andreasson gave her consent to go with the aliens. But they did not have to use force on her. There was no resisting them. Together they floated outside to the backyard, where an odd-looking, oval craft with a raised central console was waiting.

Once she was inside the craft, aliens began their examination. They used a machine that seemed to be a cross between a camera and an eye. It had a probe like a needle that was inserted into her navel. This was quite painful and Quazgaa laid his hand on her forehead to comfort her. The aliens seemed puzzled that some of her body parts were missing – she assumed that they were referring the hysterectomy she had recently undergone.

The alien's evident disappointment was later explained by UFOlogist Budd Hopkins. He believes that aliens are involved in widespread genetic sampling and are even possibly manipulating the development of humankind. Abductees frequently report sexual encounters with aliens. There are also mysterious pregnancies. Hopkins investigated the case of Kathie Davis, who had a phantom pregnancy in her teenage years. Under hypnosis she recalled that she had been abducted by aliens. Years later she had been abducted a second time and was introduced to a little girl who looked like 'an elf or an angel'. She realised that this was her baby, the half-alien, half-human hybrid that she had carried in her womb.

In another case, Collette Davis found that she was being abducted and impregnated with human–alien hybrids so often that she had a hysterectomy to protect herself from further interference.

When Betty Andreasson asked her abductors about this, she was told: 'We have to, because as time goes by, humankind will become sterile. They will not be able to reproduce.' Others believe that it is the aliens who are unable to reproduce without the involuntary assistance of humans.

During the examination, a tiny spiked ball was removed from her nostril using a long, thin instrument. For some time, this remained a puzzle. In later hypnotic sessions it emerged that Betty had been abducted before and this was some kind of device they had implanted in her.

After the examination was over, she was taken into a round room where there were eight seats that looked like armchairs. The aliens got her to sit in one of the seats and pipes were pushed into her mouth and nostrils. A clear canopy dropped down over her. The rim connected to the edge of the seat so that she was completely encapsulated. The space around her was then flooded with grey liquid. Under normal circumstances, this would have panicked her, but Andreasson was fed a spoonful of thick fluid through the pipe that went into her mouth and it seemed to have a tranquillising effect. The entire contraption began to vibrate in what she described as a very pleasant way. Then she felt herself being pushed down into the seat as if the ship were accelerating away from Earth.

When she was let out of the capsule, her clothes were sopping wet. Two hooded humanoids escorted her down a series of dark tunnels. The three of them floated along a black track. The only light was that given off by her escorts' suits. At the end of one of the tunnels she could see a mirrored wall in front of them and feared they were going to smash into it. She closed her eyes and braced herself. But there was no crash. When she opened her eyes again she found herself bathed in a vibrating infrared radiation. They passed a number of thin, lemur-like creatures that clambered on strange-looking buildings that had no glass in their windows. The creatures had suckers instead of fingers and they had two large eyes on the end of stalks that swivelled around as she passed.

The track then passed through a circular membrane and they travelled into a place that was green and beautiful like Earth. Overhead there were elevated walkways criss-crossing the sky and, in the distance, she could see cities with huge domes. Then she saw a large object silhouetted against a bright light directly ahead. As they approached it, she could see that it was a statue of an eagle, about fifteen feet high. Then, as she and her escorts stood before it, it was engulfed in flames.

When the statue had burned down to ashes, a thick, grey worm appeared in the embers. It communicated telepathically with her. She heard the words 'You have seen and you have heard. Do you understand?' in her mind. She replied that she was completely confused. But the voice spoke in her head said simply: 'I have chosen you... I have chosen you to show the world.' As a deeply religious person, Betty Andreasson believes that the voice she heard was the voice of God.

The worm then gave her a message to take back to humankind. But it was in an alien language. She was then returned to the alien ship and taken back to Massachusetts. She was still puzzled about the message that the worm had given her, but Quazgaa translated it for her. The worm had warned that humankind was following a perilous course, love was the answer and humans needed to seek out wisdom through the spirit. As they parted, Quazgaa told Andreasson that other humans had similar messages locked in their minds.

Sceptics have dismissed Andreasson's story as a hallucination brought on by the stress of her husband's hospitalisation and filtered though her own religious convictions. But that does not account for what her father saw. Later, her daughter Becky also went through regressional hypnosis and recovered memories of her mother's abduction. She said that after the aliens arrived in their home she managed to shake off the trance for a few moments. The strange visitors she saw were hairless, with pear-shaped heads and almond eyes. Their noses and ears had no external structures and the mouths were simply slits. These features are typical of Greys. She also noted that their skin was clay-like, rather than scaly, and that they had three thick fingers on their club-shaped hands. Then she lapsed back into unconsciousness.

After her hypnosis, Andreasson underwent psychiatric tests to make sure that she was not suffering from any sort of mental disorder. She also passed lie-detector and voice-stress tests. Like some other abductees, Betty Andreasson found that her life changed for the better after her experience. She became a talented artist and produced detailed drawings of what she had undergone at the hands of the aliens. Then, in 1987, she discovered a strange indented scar on her calf. Just over a year later, Raymond E. Fowler, the man who had been documenting her case, found a similar scar on his leg. Such marks are commonly found on abductees. Budd Hopkins says that they are due to cell sampling performed by aliens.

Betty Andreasson has had other encounters with aliens. During one powerful encounter, her husband John reported that mysterious black helicopters passed over their house. They were unmarked and seemed to shimmer in and out of reality. Calls to nearby airports and military bases drew a blank.

Spacenapping

Alien abductions hit the headlines again after a bizarre 'spacenapping' on 5 November 1975. That evening, Mike Rogers and his crew of six forestry workers were heading home to Snowflake, Arizona. They were heading down a track in the Heber forest when Alan Dalis, one of the crew, spotted a strange glow through the trees. As the truck moved closer, they noticed a ball of light hovering about twenty feet above the ground.

Travis Walton UFO abductee

'When we got around the trees, we all saw the source of the light – boom – less than hundred feet away, a metallic disc hovering in the air, glowing,' forestry worker Travis Walton recalled.

As the truck screeched to a halt, Travis Walton jumped out to investigate. While his more cautious friends remained in truck, the impetuous Walton approached the mysterious object. The light appeared to be about twenty feet across and was hovering in an unsteady, wavering manner, and giving off beeping and rumbling sounds.

The object was casting a circle of light on the ground. Walton stopped at the edge. He was standing almost directly underneath the object when his nerve snapped. As he turned to run back to the truck he heard a crackling sound and felt what he described as 'a numbing shock… like a high-voltage electrocution'.

Mike Rogers, the crew boss, who was still in the trunk, saw a blue-green 'bolt of energy' flash from the object and zap Walton on his back.

UFO abductee Travis Walton (centre) and Mike Rogers (right).

It picked him up and flung him back down on the ground. At this point, Rogers panicked. He floored the accelerator and drove away. A short distance down the road, he regained his composure. The other men persuaded Rogers to drive back to pick up Walton, who they had left for dead. They got there just in time to see the space-craft rise rapidly into the sky and disappear. Walton was nowhere to be seen.

The crew reported the events to the authorities in Heber. A search revealed nothing and the police suspected that Walton had been murdered by his workmates. The men were asked to take a lie detector test to clear their names. The first polygraph test was inconclusive, but a second confirmed they were telling the truth about what they had seen.

After five days and a massive police search, there was still no sign of Walton. Then suddenly, on 10 November, Walton's brother-in-law received a phone call from him. He went to collect Walton and found him naked in a phone booth a few miles outside town. Walton was seriously dehydrated, delirious, dazed, distraught and half-dead. It was only after months of rehabilitation that he was able to remember fragments of what had happened. He remem-bered being hit by the bolt of lightning and knocked out. When he regained consciousness, he found himself inside some sort of spaceship.

'I was lying on a table,' he said. 'I saw several strange creatures standing over me. I became completely hysterical and flipped out. I knocked them away, but I felt so weak I collapsed. They forced me back on the table, placed a mask over my face and I blacked out.'

The aliens were 'foetus-like', about five feet tall with domed, hairless heads, large dark eyes, tiny ears and noses, a slit for a mouth and marshmallowy skin. And they performed various exper-iments on him. He saw a humanoid entity, who showed him around but did not answer his questions. They visited a control room where he could see out through the exterior of the craft and gaze at the stars. Afterwards he lost consciousness again and when he came to he was lying on a country road near Heber.

With Six Other Witnesses

Walton Claims UFO Sighting

By JON HALVORSEN
Associated Press Writer

Travis Walton was cutting trees for $6 an hour in the forests of northern Arizona when he saw the light, a bluish-green ray that he and six witnesses say knocked him to the ground.

Three months after what he says was an encounter with an unidentified flying object, Walton says it is still difficult to lead a normal life.

At dusk last Nov. 5, as Walton tells the story, he was struck by the ray of light from a UFO in the forest and taken off in the spacecraft by strange creatures. He was missing for five days until, his family said, they found him slumped in a phone booth in Heber, Ariz., pale and shaken.

In the days that followed, reporters from as far away as Australia pursued the Walton story; psychiatrists interviewed him; UFO groups studied the incident; and Navajo County Sheriff Marlin Gillespie, whose the sheriff's department.

Walton, 23, now unemployed and living alone in a rented house in Snowflake, Ariz., says that he's barely existing financially. He has considered finishing his college education at Northern Arizona University, where he completed one year, or seeking a job in electronics.

But the tall, slender, young man says he has kept busy in recent weeks, he said, he has:
— Been "working with an artist to reproduce some of the things I've seen and writing a book" about the incident, tentatively entitled "The Walton Experience."

ON QUIZ SHOW

— Traveled to Toronto for a "news quiz show" on television and to Hollywood to film a TV pilot called "The Unexplained," in which he was interviewed by Leonard Nimoy, the pointy-eared Mr. Spock of "Star Trek" fame.
— Passed a lie-detector test about the UFO incident.

who were with him Nov. 5, passed a polygraph test about what they saw; the test on the sixth man proven inconclusive.

Mike Rogers, 28, who passed the test, is one of Walton's closest friends. Rogers still insists he saw the UFO. He says he and the others saw it as they drove along a bumpy mountain road about 12 miles south of Heber. Walton jumped out of the moving truck, ran toward the brightly glowing object hovering about 15 feet above the ground in a small clearing. He was knocked down by a ray of bluish-green light, Rogers said.

Rogers, who said he and the other men were still sitting in the truck about 25 yards away, drove off in fright. When the men returned 15 minutes later, there was no trace of Walton or the UFO, Rogers said.

Rogers, a father of four who was the foreman of the wood-cutting crew, said in words similar to Walton's: "I would prefer people to believe me, but be room."

Walton said he walked down a hallway into another room where he saw a chair with buttons on the side. He began playing with the buttons and saw a large screen filled with stars.

"In the popular TV series "Star Trek" the control room of the "Starship Enterprise" has seats with buttons on their sides and a large viewing screen often filled with stars.

Next, says Walton, a human-like creature entered the room, took him by the elbow and led him into another room where three men and a woman were standing, he said.

Walton said the creatures placed him in a chair, and from that point on he could remember nothing until he woke up in the phone booth.

Sheriff Gillespie said he became skeptical when Walton failed to show up for a lie-detector test the sheriff had arranged with the Arizona Department of Public Safety.

Contemporary newspaper clipping on the Travis Walton UFO abduction case of 5 November 1975.

What is significant about the Travis Walton case is that it is one of the few abductions observed by independent witnesses – his workmates saw his initial encounter with the UFO. It is also unusual because Walton was missing for five days. In most contemporary cases, the abduction experience lasts for only a few hours.

Over the years, sceptics have tried to debunk Walton's claims. The rarity of abduction reports in the 1970s meant Walton and his friends were subjected to years of ridicule and accusations of trickery. Yet all the men subsequently passed more lie-detector tests and the case has withstood years of rigorous investigation.

Walton recounted his abduction in the book *Fire in the Sky*, which was made into a TV film of the same name. Since the film Travis has passed two more lie-detector tests, but he has refused to be hypnotically regressed as he fears it will bring out too many disturbing memories.

Researchers are certain that Travis Walton was not suffering from any mental illness when he was abducted. It is also unlikely that all six of Walton's colleagues would have had hallucinations of the same kind at the same time. And the lie-detector tests show that they believed they saw Walton being zapped by a UFO.

More than twenty years later Walton is still clear about what happened to him.

'Something like that doesn't just disappear with the years,' he says. 'You can still remember the emotions. You can still remember the fear. When you try to cope with something like that you try to take a positive element from it. But I would rather it had not happened to me.'

To cope, he has avoided studying other cases. But he believes that some are definitely not genuine.

'I find this frustrating as it detracts from the legitimate case,' he says.

French Farce

One of the most troubling alien abduction cases took place in France on 26 November 1979. That Monday, eighteen-year-old Franck Fontaine, a street trader from the Parisian suburb of Cergy-Pontoise, disappeared in the early hours of the morning. Two of Fontaine's friends, Salomon N'Diaye and Jean-Pierre Prevost, rang the police and told them he was missing – and that they had seen a UFO shortly before he vanished.

Under interrogation, they told the whole story. On the night of the abduction, the three friends had slept for just a few hours at Prevost's high-rise flat in Cergy-Pontoise. In the morning, they planned to sell clothes in a Paris street market. The market was busy and you had to get there early to get a stall. So that morning they got up 3:30 a.m. and started loading their car.

Their ageing Ford Taunus was not the most reliable of cars. After they had brought the first load of clothes down from the flat, they decided to bump-start it. When the engine was running, they left Fontaine at the wheel to make sure it did not stall, while N'Diaye and Prevost went back up upstairs to get the rest of the gear.

While N'Diaye and Prevost were up in the flat, Fontaine spotted a bright, cylindrical light in the sky. He pointed it out to his friends when they returned to the car. There was a ready market for UFO pictures and N'Diaye reckoned that could sell a photograph to the local press at the very least. N'Diaye and Prevost went back up to the flat to find a camera, leaving Fontaine at the wheel of the car outside.

But when the two men reached the apartment, they heard the sound of the car driving away. They ran to the window and saw Fontaine drive up the road. Then, the engine cut out and the car came juddering to a halt.

N'Diaye and Prevost ran back downstairs. When they reached the street, they saw the back end of the car enveloped in a ball of glowing mist. Then a beam of light appeared from nowhere. It grew into the cylindrical shape they had seen earlier. The ball of mist then entered the hovering cylinder, which shot into the sky and vanished.

N'Diaye and Prevost ran to the car to see whether their friend Fontaine was all right. But when they reached the vehicle there was no sign of Fontaine. They looked up and down the road and searched the cabbage field beyond, but there was no trace of him. At this point Prevost grew concerned for Fontaine's safety and N'Diaye called the police. Local police made a thorough search, but neither hide nor hair of the missing Fontaine was found.

The police were more than a little bemused by Prevost and N'Diaye's story. They contacted the gendarmerie, the branch of the French police force charged with investigating UFO sightings. Meanwhile, the story leaked to the media and TV crews, and newspaper reporters from around the world descended on Cergy-Pontoise, eager to get the low-down on the latest UFO abduction.

Inside the police station, the pair were subjected to repeated interrogations – both by the local police who could not rule out the possibility of foul play, and the gendarmerie, who handled it as an alien abduction case. Eventually, Commandant Courcoux, head of the Cergy gendarmerie, emerged to tell the waiting newshounds that there were no grounds for disbelieving the two men's story. There was no doubt that something strange had happened, he said. But he had no idea what it was.

When N'Diaye and Prevost were finally released, they were besieged by reporters. Over the course of the next week, they told their story over and over again. But the constant retelling gave no new clue to Fontaine's whereabouts. And as time went by the mystery deepened.

On 3 December, seven days almost to the minute after his disappearance, Fontaine reappeared to find himself in the middle of a media circus. He had no idea that he had been missing for a week and had no recollection of what had happened to him. He thought he had simply fallen asleep for a few hours and was amazed to find himself the centre of media attention.

The story had been hot news, not just in France, but around the world. The British tabloids did not take it seriously, of course. They treated it like something straight out of a science-fiction comic. But even *The Times* carried the story. On the day after Fontaine's return, it ran the headline: 'Frenchman Back to Earth with a Bump.' The story, too, was slightly jokey. No one, it seemed, was quite sure whether to take it seriously or not.

Fontaine's reappearance failed to shed any further light on the mystery. He had woken up in the cabbage field next to the road, which both his friends and the police had searched thoroughly. He assumed that he had fallen asleep and his friends had left him. He went to Prevost's apartment, but found no one at home. Then he went to N'Diaye's place. When he rang the bell, a drowsy N'Diaye opened the door. It was N'Diaye who, to Fontaine's amazement, told him that he had been missing for seven whole days.

When they informed the police that Fontaine had returned, they took him in for questioning. But, as Fontaine had no recollection of what had happened to him, there was no way that they could progress the investigation. And, as no crime had been committed, they dropped the case. The papers soon grew tired of the story too. However, the interest of UFO groups had been tweaked and their investigations had only just begun.

The first group was the *Institut Mondial des Sciences Avancés* (World Institute of Advanced Sciences), run by French science-fiction writer Jimmy Guieu. Author of two books about UFOs and facinated by the Cergy-Pontoise case, Guieu took the three men under his wing. He whisked them off to a secluded spot, sat them down and started piecing together the definitive account of Fontaine's abduction. With four months later, Guieu's book, *Cergy-Pontoise UFO Contacts*, was on the bookshelves. It was an instant bestseller.

Guieu had taken the three friends away so that other UFOlogists could not question them, so he was accused of hogging the case. In a mixture of jealousy and pique, other UFO groups criticised Guieu's book, saying it was far from objective. While the *Institut Mondial des Sciences Avancés* found no flaws in the story told by Fontaine, N'Diaye and Prevost, a rival French UFO group called Control began to pick up on inconsistencies. The group produced a fifty-page report damning the book.

Most complaints were trifling. Although the three men said that they had been alone in Prevost's apartment on the night of the abduction, Control's Michel Piccin and other researchers discovered that Prevost's girlfriend Corrine had also been present, along with Fabrice Joly, another friend. Control also discovered that no one else in the block at night had heard the UFO, although they had heard the car being bump-started at around 4 a.m. and they had heard its engine running outside for the next few minutes. Residents returning home in the early hours had seen two people in the Ford Taunus, when Fontaine said that he had been alone. They also picked holes in the three men's chronology of the events of that night.

The account of Fontaine's return also seemed to be riddled with inconsistencies. Control said that, from the published accounts, N'Diaye seems to have been in two places at one time. But some of these apparent contradictions could just be the result of a faulty memory, and, without access to the three principal witnesses, Control had no opportunity to clear them up.

However, the major problem with the book, as far as most readers were concerned, was its lack of a first-hand account of what had happened to Fontaine during the week he had been missing. Despite Guieu's pleading, he stubbornly refused to undergo regressional hypnosis.

The rivalries between the three friends then surfaced. Prevost began writing his own account of the abduction and underwent regressional hypnosis, only to discover that it was he, and not Fontaine, who the aliens were after. After Fontaine's abduction, he had been contacted by the aliens independently. Shortly after Fontaine's return, Prevost had been visited by a mysterious 'salesman' who had taken him on a trip of Bourg-de-Sirod, a village near the Swiss border that Prevost has visited as a child. Prevost was taken to a disused railway tunnel, which led to a secret alien base. In the base, he met a group of people from every country in the world. An alien being named Haurrio told the group that they had been chosen to spread the philosophy of the aliens on Earth. They were then given a tour of the base by a beautiful female alien. Prevost slept at the base that night, but whether he slept with the alien he is too discreet to say. The next day the mysterious 'salesman' took him home.

Prevost published his account in *The Truth About the Cergy-Pontoise Affair*. He claimed that he has been chosen as the channel though which alien contacts would be made. Few people could take Prevost's fantastical claims seriously and they began to undermine the credibility of the original story.

Fontaine struck back. Although he had refused to undergo regressional hypnosis, some memories of what had happened during his week as an abductee began to seep back into his conscious mind. It all seemed like a strange, disturbing dream, but he remembered being taken into a large room and being told to lie on a small couch. The walls were lined with machinery, and two glowing spheres talked to him about the problems confronting the Earth and their solutions. Sadly, he could remember none of the details. So Fontaine decided to arrange another meeting with the aliens. On 15 August 1980, a group of UFO enthusiasts gathered in Cergy-Pontoise for the encounter. But, sadly, no one had informed the aliens and they did not turn up.

By 1983, Prevost was the leader of his own UFO group and was giving lectures on the abduction across the country. In an effort to snooker Fontaine, Guieu and the *Institut Mondial des Sciences Avancés*, he confessed that Fontaine's abduction had been a hoax.

The three young men had simply concocted the story as a money-making exercise, he said. But there was a problem with this. Neither Prevost, nor anybody else, has been able to explain where Fontaine had been during the missing week.

Nor has anyone been able to explain why the first policemen on the scene had also reported seeing some kind of 'mist' surrounding the Ford Taunus. How had Prevost, Fontaine and N'Diaye created this elaborate effect to corroborate their story?

Respected French UFOlogist Jacques Vallee, who has written a number of well received books on UFOs, has put forward another theory altogether. He says that, as part of an exercise in social control, the French military snatched Fontaine, drugged him and kept him 'in an altered state of high suggestibility' for a week. The aim was to create a religion based on UFO visitations. The programme has since been dropped, but its existence had been confirmed by Vallee's contacts inside the French Air Force, he says. Unfortunately, Vallee has not been able to offer any more corroboration, but to UFOlogists this story is all too familiar. UFO researchers in the UK and US have often found ties between the UFO phenomena and the military and intelligence communities. It is not beyond the realms of possibility that the same thing is happening in France. In that case, Prevost's confession cannot be taken at face value, but rather should be seen as part of a cleverly orchestrated campaign of disinformation.

Even though the Cergy-Pontoise abduction case has muddied the waters, the gendarmerie continues to play a central role in UFO cases. Its officers are used as preliminary investigators in the field. They are trained in how to carry out UFO investigations, paying particular attention to details that might be of interest to scientists, the effects felt by witnesses and any anomalous behaviour by wildlife in the area. When UFOs land, all traces left by the craft and samples of soil and vegetation from the area are collected and sent for analysis. The police also check the site for radioactivity and take aerial photographs of the area using a helicopter equipped with infrared cameras. The French government also funds a small UFO research programme that employs a number of top scientists.

'By virtue of the gendarmerie's presence throughout the whole territory of France,' writes Captain Kervendel in the international journal *Gendarmerie*, 'its knowledge of places and people, its integrity and intellectual honesty and the rapidity with which the gendarmerie can be on the spot, they are well place indeed to serve as a valuable auxiliary in the search for the truth about UFOs.'

Abducted from Birth

Jason Andrews seems to have been selected for alien abduction from birth, on 2 July 1983. Even as a baby, he seemed to be in the power of some strange external force. His mother, Ann, would find him on the floor under his cot when he was far too young to climb out of it. Once, she found him behind the bedroom door on the other side of the room. It was a heart-stopping moment.

The only reasonable explanation was that his three-year-old brother Daniel was responsible. He denied it and there were several occasions when Jason was moved and Daniel was not even in the house. Then, after a few months, the strange events stopped and Ann soon forgot about them. But then they were to return with a vengeance.

On Jason's fourth birthday, Ann and Jason's father, Paul, were at home with the children in their small cottage in Kent. Late in the evening, they were disturbed by a loud banging. At first it seemed to come from the doors, then from the windows, then the whole house seemed to be wracked by it. Paul though that someone was playing a practical joke on them. He opened the front door and looked out, but there was nobody there. Growing increasingly disturbed, he tried to call the police, but the phone was dead. Then a violent thunderstorm broke. Frightening though this was, it did offer some sort of explanation. But with the first crack of thunder Jason, who had been asleep on the sofa, sat bolt upright and began reeling off a series of numbers in a strange mechanical voice.

And it was not just numbers. He spewed out complex mathematical expressions, making references to pi and binary numbers – even though he had trouble counting up to ten in his picture books. Then he got up and walked to the door.

'They're waiting for me, I have to go,' he said.

Paul stopped him. It was a struggle. Jason seemed to be in a trance and was hell bent on going outside. Eventually Jason snapped out it and, when he came back to normal, he remembered nothing about his strange behaviour. Soon after, the phone began to work again. Ann and Paul called the police. But when they arrived at the house, they could find no trace of anything untoward. After the storm the cottage was surrounded by a sea of mud. If someone outside had been playing a practical joke, they would have left footprints, the police reasoned. There were none to be found.

The mysterious events of Jason's fourth birthday heralded a spate of strange new occurrences. Jason was apprehensive at bedtime. When his parents put him down for the night, he told them that small creatures came for him in the hours of darkness. In the morning, he woke tired. Often, inexplicably, he was covered in mud. And sometimes he had small scars and marks on his body. These mysteriously disappeared in a few hours.

He suffered mysterious stomach pains and was rushed into hospital twice. Once a doctor asked Ann about an operation Jason had had. She said that he had never been operated on. The doctor gave her a strange look. There was a fresh surgical scar on Jason's side. The following day it had disappeared.

At home, Ann and Paul would overhear Jason babbling in a strange language while he was alone in his bedroom. More worrying was the continued disturbance to his sleep. In the mornings, they would find him sleeping in odd places around the house. Once, they found him lying flat out on the kitchen worktop. Another time, they found him outside in the garden shed. Bafflingly, all the doors and windows of the house were locked and the shed door was bolted from the outside.

Other strange events began to plague them. Bright lights were seen over their farm, and strange figures were seen in the surrounding fields and woods. They became convinced that someone was watching the house. Then things took a more sinister turn. Their cattle died mysteriously. The vet blamed a virulent outbreak of salmonella. One of the horses on the Andrews' farm had a neat flap cut into its flank. It was a huge wound, but there was very little blood. The horse seemed docile and unconcerned. When the vet arrived, he said that the animal must have been tranquillised, and managed to sew up the wound without an anaesthetic.

The farm cat was found dead, stretched out on a bale of hay in the barn. It had a round hole bored in its head. Again, there was no blood around the wound. A few months later, a fox was found in the fields with similar hole in its head. Then four dead mice were found lined up by a farm gate, each with a small hole in its forehead and other surgical mutilations.

It was only in the autumn of 1995, when Jason was twelve, that they found out what was going on. One evening the family was watching television together. A man came on talking about how he had experienced a period of 'missing time' in his life. He told of how a thirty-five-minute journey had mysteriously taken over three hours. Since then he had suffered from uncontrollable mood swings, depression, and an irrational fear of the dark. In his efforts to find a cure, he visited a hypnotherapist who helped him to recover his memory of the lost time. At this point, Jason leapt to his feet, grabbed an ornament and threw it at the TV. The man was stupid to want to find out, he shouted. He knew what was going on, he said, and he wished he didn't.

When his parents managed to calm him down, he told them that he was being abducted by aliens. Despite the TV show, neither Paul nor Ann would accepted this. They thought Jason was simply having bad dreams. Although they were sceptical, they thought it would do no harm to look into it. They bought a few books on alien abductions and quickly realised that Jason's behaviour exactly fitted that of an abductee. For Jason, this was a breakthrough. At last, his parents believed him.

They turned for professional help to Tony Dodd, the Director of Investigations for Quest International, a body set up to investigate UFO activity. As an ex-police sergeant, Dodd was well trained to investigate such a case. He came to the conclusion that Jason was indeed an abductee, but he was unusual in that he had a conscious memory of the abductions. In most cases, the memories surfaced only under regressional hypnosis. As Dodd's investigation continued, Ann began to recover memories of abductions of her own. Like Jason, she had a memory of being in a crowd of humans who were being shown images on a large large screen of the Earth blowing up. This is a recurrent theme in abduction cases. One of the reasons, it seems, that aliens have come to Earth is to teach abductees about the destructive nature of humankind.

In the next three years, more memories came flooding back. Both Jason and Ann had memories of aliens carrying out weird medical examinations on them. A miscarriage she suffered in August 1989, she believed, was the deliberate abduction of the foetus from her womb by the aliens. On the night of the miscarriage, Ann was in such a deep sleep that Paul feared for her life.

But the aliens' interventions are not always so sinister. Jason says they are with him at other times – like when he is riding a horse or a bike – as if they are trying to share his emotions. Once, when he was thrown by a horse, he said that they hated the pain he suffered.

Dodd pointed out that Ann and Jason were reporting two common aspects of alien interest in the human race, according to the literature. They seemed to be carrying out genetic experiments on humans, perhaps harvesting human DNA. But they were also fascinated by human emotions. Observing more than one generation on the same family is also a familiar pattern.

Jason was visited by various types of aliens. His mother made a sketch from his description of those who regularly came to abduct him. Her picture shows a classic Grey, with large, black, almond-shaped eyes and a bulbous head. Other alien visitors hid themselves under hoods and cloaks, while some were humanoid. Although Jason continued to be frightened at night when he felt they were coming for him, he coped much better after his parents accepted the situation. The aliens did not seem to wish him any harm and they always returned him in the morning.

However, Jason's abductions left him tired. This resulted in behavioural difficulties at school and attracted the attention of the authorities. The social services were called in. But when the family were seen by social workers, they accepted that Jason was loved and well cared for. He was referred to a psychiatrist, who saw him for over a year and declared that he was not suffering from delusions. Others have suggested that Jason was suffering from some strange sleep disorder. But this would not explain how a small boy got out of a locked house and threw the bolt on the outside of a shed door when he was on the inside.

Ann and Paul were not people inclined to flights of fantasy. They made very credible witnesses. Their major concern was the wellbeing of their child, and supporting his abduction story, if they did not believe it to be true, would not be in his best interests.

It is hard to see what Jason would have to gain from making up such a story – and sticking to it. It attracted teasing and name-calling at school. When he confided in friends, he was called 'ET' and 'spaceboy'. What is more, there was physical evidence that supports his abduction story – the strange lights over the farm, the scars and the animal mutilations.

Experienced UFO investigator Tony Dodd was convinced.

'Jason began reporting these even when he was very young, far too young to have picked up ideas from TV or newspapers,' Dodd said. 'His parents are good witnesses. Although Ann has also been involved, Paul has no personal experience and is by nature a sceptic. But he has seen so much evidence that he accepts that his family are telling the truth.'

Dodd knows only too well the difficulties that abductees experience in getting themselves believed.

'At one time, people who said they were being abducted were regarded as cranks. But more and more people are reporting experiences similar to Jason's. They can't all be making it up. I believe the aliens are interested in studying DNA and using our genetic material in breeding experiments. They are certainly monitoring us – they may even be responsible for the Earth being inhabited in the first place.'

At fifteen, Jason was still suffering regular abductions. They came in waves, perhaps three over a couple of weeks, then nothing for two or three months. The longest break between them was six months. They follow a familiar pattern. He wakes to hear all the family's dogs barking. It is always about 3 a.m. – he checks the time on his digital clock. Suddenly the dogs fall silent, as if they have been switched off. Then a tall alien rises up at the end of Jason's bed, as if he has come up through the floorboards. Several smaller aliens are standing around the bed, but Jason does not see where they come from. Then he blacks out. He does not remember anything until he is in a strange room. He is lying on a cold, hard surface, like a marble slab. There is a bright light, although he cannot see the source. The aliens are all around him and the tall one usually has a long, thin probe in his hand. The next thing he remembers is waking up at home.

On other occasions he has played with small aliens. He wants it to stop, but has never thought that they would leave him alone permanently. In the mean time, he has learned to be stoical.

'Perhaps I have been chosen,' Jason said. 'Perhaps I am special, and maybe one day I will understand, but right now I would just like it to stop. I want them to leave me alone. I want them to let me be ordinary.'

If Jason has been chosen, he is not alone. When he was fifteen, he was contacted by nineteen-year-old James Basil. A fellow abductee, Basil was discovered to have an alien device implanted in him. They had a lot to talk about.

A Night to Remember

Although some abduction victims can supply corroborating evidence, rarely has an abductee been able to photograph the alien craft that abducted him. But that is exactly what Amaury Rivera managed to do on 8 May 1988. What's more, his photograph provided proof that the US military were involved in the UFO phenomenon.

At 4:40 a.m. that night, Amaury Rivera left a nightclub in his home town of Jabo Rojo in Puerto Rico. Some musician friends had been playing there and he had taken a camera with him to photograph the band in action. As he drove home afterwards, he found himself swathed in a dense fog. He cut his speed. Even so, he lost the road and found himself in a cattle pasture. Fearing that he might hit one of the animals, he slowed to a snail's pace.

He was practically at a standstill when he heard a strange noise. Looking towards the source of the sound, he saw two strange beings approaching him. They were identical and both about three feet tall. Their skin was white and they were hairless with huge black eyes.

He tried to escape, but in his panic he hit the brake instead of its accelerator. By then, the creatures were standing directly in front of his car. The car door began to open of its own accord. Terrified, Rivera wet himself, then lost consciousness.

When he came round, he found himself still inside his car, but the car itself was inside a strange room, which had bright grey surfaces. There were several other cars parked next to his.

'I was really confused,' said Rivera. 'I thought I was in some kind of garage and I looked around for an exit sign.'

But the two small creatures he had seen in the field reappeared. They placed their hands on his forehead and he passed out again. When he came to, he found himself in a room with fourteen other people, all sitting on benches.

'Some looked like they had come straight from a party,' said Rivera. 'Next to me was a teenager without any shoes or shirt. At this point, I still didn't believe I had been abducted by aliens. Because of my Catholic upbringing, I thought the little beings were devils and I had been in a car accident, died and gone to hell.'

A tall humanoid then came into the room. He had long black hair and his skin was dark and swarthy. He was accompanied by the two smaller beings. 'He introduced himself to us, saying he was a man like us,' Rivera said, 'but he came from another planet in a distant solar system. He spoke "verbally" in accent-free Spanish.'

During the speech, Rivera found that he could not move, but he did not know whether this was through fear or if he was restrained or otherwise paralysed. Rivera began to feel uneasy and was sure that the others felt the same. But the alien reassured them that there was nothing to be afraid of. He then told them that they had been chosen because it was necessary to share some information with them. The creature then showed them a series of three-dimensional holographic projections, which warned of the terrible fate that awaited the Earth if humankind did not mend its ways.

The first projections showed a comet colliding with the Earth. It hit the Caribbean near Puerto Rico with such force that it devastated the planet. A second showed what happened to the world after this cataclysm – there would be a single world government on an artificial island in a black polluted sea. When the show was over, Rivera was rendered unconscious a third time. This time, when he awoke, he found himself back in his car, outdoors, some distance from where the abduction had begun. Next, he heard the roar of jets overhead. On looking up, he saw three jet-fighters chasing a disc-shaped UFO.

In a flash of inspiration, he remembered that he had his camera in the car. Grabbing it, he leapt out and started shooting away. Although there were three jets in pursuit, only one appears in Rivera's photographs.

'The jets would take turns circling around the UFO so that one would always be near to it,' explains Rivera. 'That is why you only see one jet with the UFO in the pictures I released.'

But Rivera had been lucky to get any pictures at all. Within seconds, the UFO took off at a fantastic speed, leaving the jets standing. Rivera was hardly able to believe the evidence of his own eyes. Fortunately, he had captured the scene on film. And a few days later, after he developed the film, he had proof that what he had seen was real.

He took the pictures to Jorge Martin, editor of the Puerto Rico's leading UFO magazine, *Evidencia OVNI*. Martin was impressed. Not only was Rivera's tale convincing – with evidence to back it up – the pictures suggested that the US military knew about UFOs, as UFOlogists had suspected.

'The Rivera case is a very impressive one because of the evidence,' said Martin. 'He was able to take pictures of the disc and include the jet interceptors. These jets have been identified as F-14 "Tom Cat" fighters, which are used by the US Navy. Many witnesses have also reported seeing the same type of jets attempting to intercept UFOs over different areas of Puerto Rico on other occasions. When you see the pictures, it is obvious that the government has been lying for decades about their involvement.'

Puerto Rico has been a UFO hotspot since 1987. The centre of the activity is Laguna Cartagena, near Cabo Rojo where Rivera was abducted, and a small mountain ridge called Sierra Bermeja. A number of witnesses had seen UFOs flying in and out of the waters of Laguna Cartagena. Indeed one local witness, a Mrs Ramirez, said that she had seen flying saucers entering the lake since 1956.

'At first, they were bright and luminous,' she said. 'As they came out you could define their shape more clearly. They were disc-shaped, with a translucent dome on top and you could see people or figures inside the domes.'

It is no coincidence that there are a number of US military establishments in Puerto Rico. More than two-thirds of the nearby island of Vieques has been occupied by the US Navy for fifty years. Despite protests from the inhabitants, they refuse to hand it back. The US government has also sealed off the area around Laguna Cartagena.

Jorge Martin says that there have been other cases of UFOs being pursued by jet fighters over Puerto Rico. On 16 November 1988, Yesenia Valasquez saw a huge ball of yellow light hovering over the town of San German. With other members of her family, she witnessed two jet fighters intercept the object and fly around it.

'Then, all of a sudden, they seemed to enter the object from below and disappeared,' she said. After that the UFO emitted two balls of light, which streaked away into the distance. The UFO followed.

Luminous pyramid-shaped craft are often seen over Puerto Rico. One of these appeared over the town of Barranquitas near the centre of the island on 18 November 1995. It hovered over the local radio station, Radio Procer, and played havoc with their electronic equipment. It was seen by numerous witnesses, but the authorities denied that anything unusual happened that day.

Because of the massive US military presence on Puerto Rico and the US government's secrecy, some UFOlogists have concluded that there is an alien base on the island, where extraterrestrials and US scientists perform secret experiments.

Rivera's photographs were sent for professional analysis. Professor Victor Quesada of the University of Mexico and Jim Dilettoso, whose Village Labs in Arizona uses state-of-the-art computer imaging technology in its consulting work for NASA, both examined the pictures and said they could find no evidence of fraud.

Their analysis showed that the disc-shaped craft and the jet were about two to two-and-a-half miles away from Rivera's position. The jet was moving at some speed, while the disc was standing still or moving slowly. In all four pictures Rivera took, the ambient light conditions were correct. This ruled out the use of models, paste-up, montages and all known forms of technical manipulation. Nothing in them contradicted anything Rivera said about what had happened when he took the photographs. As a result, they concluded that the pictures were genuine.

Jorge Martin found a fisherman named Andreas Mandolano who had also been abducted. His story exactly matched Rivera's experience. 'He told me various things like the name of the alien and other points that Rivera had only revealed to me,' said Martin. 'This, on top of the fact that the two men had never met or discussed the case, provides good corroborative evidence for Rivera's claims.'

During his investigation, Martin tracked down four people who described being abducted by the same creatures that Rivera had seen. 'It appears as if this alien has been contacting people from all around the area of Puerto Rico,' said Martin.

But according to Rivera, there were fourteen other abductees with him in the room on the alien craft. Where were the other ten? Rivera went on TV and asked for them to come forward. Several hundred people responded. Out of this group, Rivera managed to find seven who were in that room with him on the same night. Martin and Rivera are still trying to locate the other three.

The case attracted the attention of veteran American UFOlogist Wendelle Stevens. In his thirty-six years of UFOlogy, he had come to specialise in alien contact cases that involve the delivery of information. Like other investigators, Stevens was impressed by the emotion that Rivera displayed when recounting his experience – something that researchers believe is difficult to fake convincingly.

'At first, when he started to talk about his experience, he would turn pale and shake and you could see he was genuinely frightened,' says Stevens. 'You could tell he was still deeply affected by what had happened to him. He has now processed his experience sufficiently to be able to talk publicly without a high degree of trauma and with more confidence. From the evidence I have seen, there is no doubt in my mind that what he described really happened to him.'

What is more, he has four unimpeachable photographs and eleven other abductees to back his story. With such impressive evidence, it is not surprising that Amaury Rivera attracted the attention of the 'Men in Black'.

Shortly after his abduction, Rivera was visited by three black-suited men at his home in Cabo Rojo.

'They said they were from the CIA and showed me papers which had a CIA letterhead,' Rivera says. 'But I was so nervous that I wasn't able to read what was written on them. They told me it would be easier if I just gave them the photographs and negatives.' This was before Rivera and Martin had released the pictures to the press.

Rivera told them that he did not know what they were talking about, but they said they had a warrant to search his house.

'I told them "go ahead, be my guest", says Rivera. 'They searched but didn't find anything. I had hidden them far too well.'

UFOs at the UN

It is hard for the general public to believe that human beings are being abducted by aliens, and UFOlogists have long hoped that a case backed by irrefutable proof and unimpeachable witnesses would come up so that they could prove their case. And at the first Alien Study Conference at the Massachusetts of Technology on 13

June 1992, one case that had the potential to be just such a clincher was put forward.

The researcher on the case was Budd Hopkins, the New York-

Linda 'Cortile an -
abductee.

based artist and sculptor turned UFOlogist. It involved a woman, a New York housewife, known pseudonymously as 'Linda Cortile', who lived in an apartment block on the Lower East Side, just two blocks from the Brooklyn Bridge. In December 1989 Hopkins received a telephone call from an emotionally distraught Cortile. While she lay in bed on the night of 30 November 1989 about 3 a.m., the forty-one-year-old Italian-American had been approached by a 'small, grey-skinned alien'. In the presence of this creature, she felt her body became completely paralysed. She had only a vague recollection of what happened next, but she recalled lying on a table and being examined.

Mrs Cortile was so distressed that it was plain something had to

The block of flats (right background) from where Linda Cortile was alleged-ly abducted in 1989; the *New York Post* night- loading bay is on the right; Manhattan, New York, USA.

be done urgently. So on 2 December 1989 Hopkins organised a session of regressional hypnosis, which he tape-recorded. Under hypnosis, Cortile provided a full account of her experience.

She began: 'Behind the drapes. There's something there. There's someone in the room... Ooh, I can't move my arms anymore. Now one, two, three, there's four and five. They're taking me outta bed. I won't let them. I won't let them take me outta bed.'

Hopkins asked her to describe the visitors.

'They're short. They're white and dark... Their eyes. Very intense eyes... Black. They shine.'

Realising that he was dealing with classic 'Greys', Hopkins asked what happened next.

'They lift me up and they bring me to the living room... They took me to the window. And there was a bright light. Blue-white. [Inaudible] right outside. I'm outside. I'm outside the window. It's weird.'

The aliens had floated Cortile out through her twelfth-storey window, even though it was locked and covered by a metal child-guard fence. She hovered there, suspended above the street. Then the creatures levitated the helpless woman up into the belly of a waiting spaceship. Inside she found herself lying on a table where they began examining her back and her right nostril. She was then questioned about her family. Afterwards they allowed her to leave the examining table. She remembered heading for the door, but the next thing she remembered was being back in bed in her apartment.

Linda Cortile and Budd Hopkins, 1991.

By Mrs Cortile's account, there was nothing exceptional about her case. It was just one of thousands of similar abductions reported to UFO researchers the world over, and may just have rated a footnote in one of Hopkins' books. But fifteen months later, Hopkins discovered something that would make this case very different indeed – the abduction itself had been witnessed.

In February 1991, two police officers who identified themselves only as 'Richard' and 'Dan' wrote to Hopkins. Although no details of the Cortile case had been made public, in their letter, Richard and Dan recounted witnessing an abduction that matched Mrs Cortile's precisely. They said that, at 3:30 a.m. 'in late November 1989', when they sat in their car, they saw 'a strange oval hovering over the top of an apartment building... its lights turned from a bright reddish orange to a very whitish blue. It moved out away from the building and lowered itself to an apartment window just below.'

Next they saw a woman floating in mid-air in a bright beam of bluish-white light. She was followed by three ugly little human-like beings who sprang out of the window one by one, in the foetal position, before straightening out. Then, with one above her and two below, they escorted her up to the waiting UFO. Once she was on board, the oval craft turned reddish-orange again and whisked away. 'It then plunged into the river behind us, not far from pier 17, behind the Brooklyn Bridge,' they said.

The two police officers ended their letter by saying that they wanted to retain their anonymity due to their professional standing. They also mentioned that they might try to contact the female they had seen.

In *Witnessed*, Hopkins' book about the case, he wrote: 'My astonishment at reading this letter was all the more profound because I was almost certain that I knew the woman.'

Although to those outside the UFO community, the Cortile case might appear absurd, the fact that it had been observed by two unimpeachable witnesses, who had nothing to gain by coming forward, proved to any reasonable standard that it had actually happened. The problem was that Hopkins had no return address for Richard and Dan. Nor did he know their full names. So there is no way he could contact them. However, they had mentioned in their letter that they might try to contact the woman they had seen being abducted.

Hopkins was concerned that meeting them without any prior warning might have a bad effect on Mrs Cortile. So he contacted her and told her about the two men. Together, they planned what to do should Richard and Dan contact her. Two weeks later, on 19 February 1991, the two men knocked on the door of her apartment.

Although Hopkins never got to meet Richard or Dan, Mrs Cortile met them on several occasions. During their first meeting, Richard and Dan questioned her closely about her abduction, and

apologised for not coming to her assistance. Mrs Cortile sympa-
thised. The two men seemed to have been badly shaken by the
event. It seemed that they could still hardly believe that it had happened and needed confirmation.

Hopkins had asked Mrs Cortile to ask the two men to contact
him – or at least prepare a written or taped account of what they
saw. They should do this before she said too much. In this way, he
would have their account on record before it was influenced by
what she told them. They agreed to do this, and left.

The following month, Hopkins received an audiocassette from
Richard and Dan. It confirmed that they had witnessed an alien
abduction on 30 November 1989 and spelt out everything they had
seen in great detail. As police officers they were trained in observation and presenting detailed witness testimony in court. Next,
Hopkins set himself the task of tracking down the two men and
confirming their identities. This was made more difficult by
Richard and Dan's next letter, which explained that they were not
quite who they had said they were – and that a third witness, a VIP,
had been present that night.

Although Hopkins met with the so-called 'Third Man' at an air-
port in 1993 and received a package containing information on the
case from him, he has never revealed his identity. But other
UFOlogists have come to believe he was the then UN Secretary
General Javier Perez de Cuellar. The clue comes from Mrs
Cortile's regressional hypnosis. During her abduction, she recalled
seeing a car carrying diplomatic registration plates being parked
near her home. Mrs Cortile also believes she saw Dan standing
next to Russian premier Mikhail Gorbachev during a newscast
from the United Nations in December 1988. When Hopkins located the clip, she said she was '150 per cent sure' that man was Dan.

Piecing together the story, it seems that Richard and Dan were
no ordinary patrolmen, but officers assigned to guard diplomats
and other VIPs. They had been driving de Cuellar through New
York late at night when their car came to a mysterious halt on
Franklin D. Roosevelt Drive not far from the exit to Brooklyn
Bridge. It was then that they witnessed Cortile's abduction.

Hopkins has suggested that the abduction was 'a deliberate performance' put on for the benefit of a man of international standing. What better witness could you have?

But that was not the end of the story. On Monday, 29 April, Hopkins got another call from Mrs Cortile. She was very agitated. She had just been abducted again. Not by aliens this time, but by Richard and Dan.

'They forced me into their car and drove me around for about three hours just asking me questions,' she said. During this interrogation, Richard and Dan apparently accused Mrs Cortile of working for a government agency. They said she was an alien, and insisted on seeing her naked feet. On a second occasion, Dan alone abducted Mrs Cortile, took her to a beach on Long Island, and forced her to wear a night-gown similar to the one she had worn that night. He said he did this to check whether it really was Mrs Cortile he had seen on the night of the abduction. She said he also attempted to rape her. In a letter to Hopkins in September 1991, Dan explained that the Third Man had suddenly recalled being on a beach with Mrs Cortile seconds after they had seen her being abducted. Hopkins concluded that all three men had been abducted too. Apparently, the aliens were using Mrs Cortile – who they referred to as the 'Lady of the Sands' – to explain to the 'leading politician' the damage that humankind was doing to the environment. Mrs Cortile's subsequent hypnotic regressions confirmed this. And Richard had proof. The aliens had been collecting sand samples for analysis and he had managed pick up some of it while aboard the alien craft. On 20 May 1992, Richard sent Hopkins two small bags of sand. He had taken one sample from a 'contraption with metal-like pipes or tubes inside it,' Richard said. The other, contained sand he had found in his shoe. Afterwards he had put the samples away in a drawer and forgot about them.

Hopkins sent the samples to the University of Nevada for analysis. Chemically the samples were almost identical, though an electron microscope revealed that they differed considerably in grain size. The sample from the machine also had a slightly higher lead content. Hopkins could not figure out what this meant. The researchers at the University of Nevada were puzzled too. They could not figure out what they were supposed to be looking for.

Then Hopkins discovered that Richard and Mrs Cortile had both been abducted together all their lives, and that Richard may have been the father of Cortile's son. Dan apparently went insane. This made him 'an official problem' and he disappeared. This spooked Mrs Cortile, who hired a private detective to protect her.

On 20 October 1991 Mrs Cortile woke to find her face and pillow covered with blood and concluded that she had had a nosebleed during the night. She called Hopkins to tell him about it. In passing she mentioned that a week before, her niece, a chiropodist, had taken an X-ray of her head because, since childhood, she had a lump on her nose and scarring inside her nasal cavity that doctors could not account for. However, an examination of the X-ray provided the answer. There was a tiny, cylindrical object lodged up her nose. A second X-ray was taken, which showed no such object. Hopkins deduced that Mrs Cortile had been abducted again and the object had been removed – hence the nosebleed. Further hypnosis revealed that, when she had been abducted in 1975, an alien had used a long needle to insert a similar object up her right nostril. When she was regressed again in 1992, she recalled that an alien had entered her apartment on the night of the nosebleed and removed an object, which it had called a 'regulator'.

No matter how bizarre things became, more witnesses came forward to verify Mrs Cortile's abduction in November 1989. Nevertheless, sceptics still pour scorn on the case. They point out that, over the years, no one but Mrs Cortile and her family have ever seen Richard and Dan. All their communication with Hopkins has been via letter or tape. Hopkins has failed to prove that the two men exist to the sceptics' satisfaction. Perez de Cuellar has denied being in a stalled car on the night in question. And he has not admitted that he was involved in an alien abduction.

Sceptics also point out that if Mrs Cortile had been abducted by a huge illuminated UFO hovering over FDR Drive, even at 3:30 in the morning, there should have been thousands of witnesses. The freeway would have been littered with stalled cars, but the event did not even make the newspapers. Neither the workers at the near-by loading bay of the *New York Post* nor the 24-hour security staff at Mrs Cortile's apartment block reported seeing a UFO.

Hopkins' integrity is above question. No one would suggest that he would fake a case. So the sceptics have no choice but to point the finger of suspicion at Mrs Cortile, and Hopkins is merely being a dupe. UFO sceptic Philip Klass says: 'Hopkins does not consider the possibility that the Dan and Richard letters were authored by Mrs Cortile herself.' But Hopkins sympathises with witnesses like Richard and Dan who are reluctant to go public 'especially when you get someone like Philip Klass waiting in the wings to pounce when they come out; it's witness harassment... blatantly dishonest and cruel'.

Klass was also suspicious that each new revelation by Richard and Dan was immediately confirmed by Mrs Cortile under hypnosis. But Hopkins points out that there is not a shred of evidence of a conspiracy. If Mrs Cortile was the lynch pin of a huge hoax, her co-conspirators would have to have included her young sons, Stephen and John, and her husband Steve, who all met Richard and could describe his physical appearance. Somehow she would also have had to co-opt 'Janet Kimball', the pseudonym of another eye-witness who claimed to have seen the abduction, and Lisa Bayer, her niece, the chiropodist who took the X-rays of the alien implant found in her nose, and a number of other friends and neighbours.

'The basic rule for a scam is you don't have a cast of thousands,' says Hopkins. 'Besides, how could it be maintained for so long?'

The Third Man, whoever he was, also plied Mrs Cortile and her family with expensive gifts – which had to be paid for. A hoax would also have required detailed planning, Oscar-winning acting and the ability to memorise complex narratives and descriptions.

As Mrs Cortile points out: "It would take Bobby Fischer [US chess grandmaster] to come up with this hoax. Only one per cent of people have a Bobby Fischer mind, so I should take it as a compliment.'

She accuses her denigrators of being not sceptics but debunkers. 'If a person is intelligent but has a closed mind, they can't learn anything. That makes them a moron,' she says. On the other hand, 'this isn't something anyone wants to believe – especially me.'

'Scepticism is fine,' says Hopkins. 'I approach all my new cases as a sceptic – but most sceptics will hear fifty pieces of supporting evidence but look at the fifty-first and find something about it that makes them sweep the rest of the evidence away.'

Mrs Cortile's abductions stopped in 1993. She thinks this was because she was getting older and no longer has the eggs that her abductors were looking for. By that time she was no longer convinced that the UFO that abducted her was manned by extraterrestrials. She had come to believe that her abduction could have been a military experiment and points out that there is a military base not far away on Governor's Island. This was where the 'Third Man's' car was headed, she thinks.

Communion

It is the night after Christmas Day 1985. Before going to bed, a man sets the alarm and locks the doors of his house in the country, a couple of hours' drive north of New York City. He retires for the night earlier than usual, but in the small hours of the morning a disturbance wakes him. He sits up in bed, but the panel in the bedroom shows that no burglar alarm has been tripped.

He wonders whether to get dressed and take a look outside. The snow-covered grounds around the house might show footprints. But he finds himself stricken with fear. Sleep seems out of the question, but he relaxes and gradually begins to drift off. Suddenly he is awoken again by a strange noise. He senses a presence in the room. In panic, he reaches for the light switch. As he moves, he sees a shape flying towards him at incredible speed.

The freezing temperature outside brings him around, but he still feels as if he is in a dream. There are strange creatures all around him. Suddenly he feels a tremendous sensation of acceleration and sees the forest floor receding below him. Then he blacks out again.

Next time he awakes, he finds himself in a small, foul-smelling circular room. A strange being – hairless, thin and about five feet tall – appears. There is barely a trace of a nose or a mouth, but its eyes are mesmerising. They are bulging, slanted and as black as night.

Without warning, a needle is inserted into the man's brain. A cut is made in his forefinger and he is given by a painful anal probe. The next thing he knows, he is all alone in the forest in the morning sunlight.

Is this story familiar? It should be. It is an account of the abduction of Whitley Strieber, whose book – and subsequent film – *Communion* made him the world's most famous abductee. In the book, he claims to be the victim of multiple abductions. In fact, his whole life is plagued by little bug-eyed aliens stomping around his home at night and whisking him off for proctology practice.

Author and abductee Whitley Strieber, photographed in July 1997 at Roswell UFO Encounter 1997.

Strieber was born in San Antonio, Texas, the son of a wealthy lawyer. As a child, he was fascinated by the space race and once, as a joke, his school friends painted him green. He was always talking about little green men. He graduated from the University of Texas and went to film school in London. Then he moved back to New York where he worked in advertising, though he spent much of his free time studying witchcraft and mysticism.

In his thirties, he decided to become a writer and in 1978 he published *The Wolfen*, which was about a pack of super-wolves who roam Manhattan, ripping people's throats out. It was made into a movie. The book was followed by *The Hunger* about a romance between a couple of high-school vampires. He continued in the vein of horror-thriller with supernatural overtones. In one book, *Cat Magic*, the female protagonist is abducted by fairies –

small humanoids who have 'sharp faces with pointed noses and large eyes'. They take great delight in examining her both physically and mentally.

Another trend in his fiction was the claim that his books were true stories, though related by fictional characters. But in the futuristic book *Warday*, which Strieber co-wrote with James Kunetka, the two authors wrote as themselves, only fictionalising their future experiences in the book. So the line between fact and fiction had become well and truly blurred.

Then it happened. On 4 October 1985 Strieber, his wife Anne and their son Andrew, along with their friends Jacques Sandulescu and Annie Gottlieb, who were both writers, went to stay in the Striebers' cabin in upstate New York for the weekend. That night, it was foggy and Strieber lit the stove. He woke to find a blue light shining on the ceiling. He was frightened. The cabin was out in the woods and he could not see the headlights of passing traffic. In his sleepy state, it passed through his mind that the chimney might be on fire. Then he fell back into a deep sleep.

Later he was awoken by a loud bang. It woke his wife and he could hear his son downstairs shouting. When he opened his eyes he found the cabin was shrouded in a glow that extended out into the fog. He cursed himself for falling back asleep. Now the roof was on fire. He told his wife that he would go and get their son. She should wake the others. But before he could get downstairs the glow suddenly disappeared. In the morning, Jacques Sandulescu mentioned that he had been bothered by a light the night before, but nothing more was said.

Later that week Strieber found himself increasingly disturbed by the incident. Then he suddenly remembered seeing a huge crystal, hundreds of feet tall, standing on end over the house. It was emitting the strange blue glow. His wife thought he was crazy.

Slowly, in Strieber's mind, the cabin became a dark and terrible place. New York City also seemed dangerous and he decided to move back to Texas. Strieber and his wife went down to Austin in November. But when he saw the house that they intended to buy, he became paranoid. The huge Texas sky, he thought, was a living thing. And it was watching him. He cancelled the plans to move to Texas. His wife was furious. If he did not pull himself together, she said, she would leave him.

Strieber put aside his fears until they went up to the cabin again at Christmas. The night of 26 December 1985 was the night it happened. He awoke, he said, to hear a peculiar sound, as if lots of people were running around downstairs. Suddenly a small figure flew at him. He lost consciousness. Next, he got the impression that he was being carried. He awoke to find himself in a small depression out in the woods. He was paralysed and someone was doing something to the side of his head. The next thing he knew, he was travelling upwards high above the forest. He found himself in a circular room. It was messy and he was terrified. Small creatures were scurrying around him. They inserted a needle into his brain. Then they examined his rectum with a probe, possibly to take a sample of faecal matter, but leaving Strieber with the distinct impression that he was being anally raped. Then they cut his forefinger.

Strieber awoke back in his bed in the cabin. He felt a distinct sense of unease. He read a report in the newspapers about a UFO being sighted over upstate New York that night. His brother had bought him a book about UFOs for Christmas. He tried to read it but, for no reason, it frightened him. He ploughed on though. Finally he got to the chapter about alien abductions and everything began to make sense.

Back in New York City, he got the number of UFO abduction researcher Budd Hopkins from the telephone book and phoned him. Hopkins suggested that he investigate the events of the night of 4 October, as then he had witnesses. His wife remembered being awakened by the bang, but did not remember the glow. Jacques Sandulescu remembered the light, but neither of them could come up with an explanation for it. Strieber's son had the most interesting recollection. When he had heard the bang, he had been told that it was okay because his father had just thrown a shoe at a fly. 'Told by who?' he was asked.

'A bunch of little doctors,' he said. He had dreamt that a bunch of little doctors had carried him out on to the porch. They had told him telepathically that they were not going to hurt him. The boy said it was the strangest dream because it was 'just like real'.

At Hopkins' suggestion, Strieber went to see a therapist. He had been feeling suicidal. He also suggested regressive hypnosis. After a couple of weeks, Strieber dropped the therapy, but kept on with the hypnosis.

At the first session, Strieber was regressed to 4 October. He recalled seeing something flash past the window. Then came the light. He saw a goblin wearing a cloak in the corner of the bed-room. It rushed at him and struck him on the forehead with a wand. At this point, Strieber screamed so hard that he came out of the hypnotic trance. When he was put under again, he saw pictures of the world blowing up.

'That's your home,' the goblin said.

Then he saw his son in a park, an image that Strieber associated with death. The goblin said that he would not hurt Strieber. But he took a needle and lit the end. It exploded and Strieber began to think of the house burning down. It was as if the goblin had implanted the image. Then he came out of the trance again.

He went under once more to find out what happened. This time he saw his son dead in the park. Then he saw his father dying. He was sitting in an armchair choking while his mother watched. This was not the scene as his mother described it.

In a later session, Strieber was regressed to 26 December. He recalled being dragged naked from his bedroom by aliens in blue overalls. They dragged him out into the woods and sat him on a chair, which, with a whoosh, propelled him hundreds of feet in the air. Next he was on a bench in a room. There was a female alien there in a tan suit. She stuck something resembling a penis up Strieber's backside and told him that he was 'the chosen one' in a flat Midwestern accent. He scoffed. Then she tried to get him to have an erection. But he could not, fully. He did not fancy her. She had leathery yellow skin and a mouth like an insect, and besides, the atmosphere was rather intimidating. The next thing he knew, he was naked on the living room couch. He went upstairs, put his pyjamas on and went to bed.

Further hypnosis revealed more bizarre abductions. One time, he was in spaceship and saw his sister in her nightie sprawled on an examination table. His father, paralysed, stood beside her. On other tables were soldiers in uniform, unconscious. He was even invited to give a lecture on the evils of the British Empire. Another time, he awoke to find a group of hybrids around his bed. The aliens seemed to be tinkering with his mind, showing him symbols and images that evoked thoughts and memories in his mind.

Outside hypnosis, Strieber's life became more and more bizarre. He woke up one night, paralysed, convinced that a probe had been shoved up into his brain via his nose. He developed nosebleeds. So did his wife and son. Strieber began to smell the odour of aliens around his apartment. Symbols the aliens had shown him appeared on his arm. He suffered the sensation of missing time regularly. He was plagued with bizarre memories and strange phone calls. His stereo began speaking to him. He became so afraid of his apartment that he moved to Connecticut. But when Connecticut proved scary too, he moved back to New York.

Numerous psychological and physical tests were run on him and no-one could find anything wrong. The answer, Strieber concluded, must lie with UFOs. Hopkins plugged him into the UFO network, but he managed to alienate Hopkins' contacts with his eccentricities. Strieber became paranoid about reporters, fearing that, if news of his abduction experiences came out, he would be held up to ridicule, which might damage his career.

Strieber began to feel that he was all written out anyway. His last book had not done well and his abduction experiences were making it impossible for him to work. He decided to confront his fears and write about the abduction itself, though he was not sure whether his experiences were real or whether they were memories from a former life. Nevertheless he produced the manuscript of a book he called *Body Terror*. But one night, when his wife was asleep beside him, she spoke to him in a strange deep voice. She warned him that he should change the title to *Communion*, otherwise he would frighten people.

Strieber circulated the manuscript. According to Hopkins, it came across as something in Strieber's horror-thriller genre, rather than a factual account. In one place, the female alien leads him around by the penis like a dog on a lead. He persuaded Strieber to tone it down a bit. Once he had done this, Strieber secured a million-dollar advance on the book. It was published in 1987, as *Communion: A True Story*. It sold millions worldwide. Strieber has since published four more books in his 'Communion' series.

The Dark Secret of Dulce

In the late 1980s UFO investigator Paul Bennewitz received a report of an alien abduction in New Mexico. At first it seemed to fit the classic abduction pattern. The majority of abduction cases begin with unaccompanied people seeing strange lights in the sky. Before they know it, they are face to face with a creature from another world. Then they are taken aboard a spacecraft, where they undergo an intimate physical examination. Afterwards, they are returned to the place they were taken from, somewhat shaken. Often they have no memory of what has happened. The only clues that something strange has occurred are mysterious marks on their bodies and the discovery that there was 'missing' time that they could not account for. And the only way what happened can be revealed is through the controversial technique of regressional hypnosis. However, when Bennewitz read further into the case, he started to suspect that the abduction was only a small part of a far greater mystery.

The abductee, Christa Tilton of Oklahoma, said that she had been kidnapped in July 1987 by two small 'Grey' aliens. Regressional hypnosis revealed that she had been forced into a saucer-shaped spacecraft. But then her story began to differ from the regular pattern. The alien craft took her to a secret hillside location. There she was handed over to a man wearing a red military-style one-piece suit. He took her down a tunnel lined with security cameras. She passed through computerised check-points, then she was put on transit vehicle which took her to another area. There she was made to stand on a device that looked like a weighing machine, though instead of a dial it had a computer screen.

Tilton was issued with an identity card, and told that she had just entered level one of an underground facility. As the ordeal continued, the terrified abductee was taken down to level five, where she saw more of the strange grey creatures that had abducted her. The facility also housed a number of spacecraft like the one that had brought her there.

In another enormous chamber she saw a series of large tanks. They smelled of formaldehyde and were linked up to computerised gauges. She had no idea what was in the tanks, but later she was able to make drawings of them. It was these drawings that impressed Paul Bennewitz. He had seen them before. Just a few months earlier, he had seen an almost identical series of sketches. These had been part of a document entitled *The Dulce Papers*, which was put together by former Dulce Base Security Officer Thomas Edwin Castello, explaining what he had seen at the top-secret facility.

3 Theories Galore

The Starchild Theory

There is a theory that aliens are conducting some genetic experiment on earth. They are taking women and impregnating them with starchildren. A typical victim is a woman, Helen, who had been having terrible encounters with UFOs and aliens for years. They had come at night since she was a child. She tried to convince herself that her nocturnal visitors were merely vivid dreams, but the time she spent in a cold room being prodded by small, grey-skinned, hairless creatures with strange, slanting eyes who probed her with strange instruments felt terribly real.

Then, one day in 1989, something different happened. Again she had been abducted at night and taken to the same cold room; this time one of her captors held a tiny baby, perhaps just a few days old. Helen took it and, when she examined it closely, she saw that it seemed to share both human and alien features. Normally she would have found its appearance repellent. Instead she was overcome with maternal feelings. She felt like a new mother being shown her child for the first time. And as she cuddled it close, the aliens close by watched in fascination.

Helen was the latest in a long line of women used by aliens in strange reproduction experiments. Men too have had semen samples taken during abductions. Some UFOlogists believe the alien visitors are trying to breed a race of hybrids – half human, half extraterrestrial.

The first clue to this came in October 1957, when the Brazilian farmer Antonio Villas-Boas was led aboard a UFO by several small, humanoid creatures, before being seduced by a beautiful female alien with bright red pubic hair. Afterwards she pointed to her belly and to the sky in a gesture that he interpreted to mean that she was going to have his baby up somewhere in out space.

Villas-Boas was rather embarrassed by the tale, and spoke of it at length only to a doctor in Rio de Janeiro, who found he was suf-

fering from mild radiation sickness. The story was not published in
Brazil for many years, but it was logged with the British UFO journal, *Flying Saucer Review*, which eventually published it in 1964.

Three weeks after Villas-Boas was abducted, a related encounter
occurred in England. There was a flash of light that left scorch
marks on an old newspaper in the Birmingham home of a young
mother, Cynthia Appleton, and an alien with long, blond hair mate-
rialised. During this visit, and several others over the coming
months, the alien told Mrs Appleton about the dangers of atomic
energy. In later visits, some of which were witnessed by Mrs
Appleton's daughter, the alien gave up its flashy entrances and
arrived in an old-fashioned suit and a dark car, as if it were a Man
in Black.

On one of these visits he told Cynthia she was pregnant. It was
a boy. He would be a fair-haired boy. The alien told her when the
baby would be born, the birth weight and the name he should be
given. Mrs Appleton dashed to her doctor, who confirmed that was
indeed pregnant and that she had conceived around the time of the
alien's first visit. After that, the blond-haired alien made one last
visit to assure Mrs Appleton that, though her son was the product
of the alien race, he had been fathered by her husband. Mr
Appleton's reaction has not been recorded.

It was later discovered that Cynthia Appleton's pregnancy was
not the first time that the aliens had brought a little bundle of joy to
Earth. In 1950, in the town of Anthony, Kansas, a young farming
couple were awoken by a UFO. They went outside to investigate
and encountered a glowing figure. It announced that the woman
was pregnant with a baby 'sent' by the aliens and that the child
would grow up to spread the word of their presence.

The woman was indeed pregnant and had a baby daughter, but
the couple decided that it was best not to tell the child of their
encounter. The girl's name was Donna Butts. She grew up unaware
of her alien ancestry, married and had a family of her own, but her
extraterrestrial heritage could not be denied. In November 1980,
while driving with her family outside Topeka, Kansas, they got
stuck behind a truck. Suddenly the sky was filled with a beam of

light. The next thing anyone knew, they were driving into Topeka itself. The miles in between seemed to have vanished miraculously.

When Donna told the story to her parents, they told her about her conception. Under regressional hypnosis, she remembered being abducted by Greys. They had told her that human civilisation was entering its 'end times' and that she was one of the alien emissaries on Earth who would help guide humankind into the new millennium. Since then, she has met up with other 'starchildren' who are the progeny of the alien's hybridisation scheme. We do not know whether Cynthia Appleton's son was one of these.

The type of blond-haired Nordic-type aliens that brought Cynthia Appleton her little surprise appeared in Latin America and confessed. On 7 August 1965, at San Pedro de los Altos, thirty miles south of Caracas in Venezuela, two businessmen and a gynaecologist were visiting a stud farm when there was a brilliant flash of light. A spherical craft drifted to the ground making a soft humming noise. Two Nordics in silver suits then got out. The men were terrified, but the aliens told them, telepathically, to be calm. They explained that they were from Orion. They had come to Earth to study the psyches of humans and adapt them to their own species and to check out the possibility of 'inter-breeding to create a new species'. What better place to start than at a stud farm?

They also explained that, while they were pretty well disposed towards human beings, there was another race of aliens – Small Greys – visiting Earth who were less benign.

The aliens' genetic agenda has in fact been plain from the outset. In the first publicised alien abduction case – that of Betty and Barney Hill in the White Mountains of New Hampshire in September 1961 – sperm samples were taken from Barney and what was termed 'a pregnancy test' attempted on Betty. After that there was a tidal wave of alien contacts, all of which involved intimate examinations and genetic experimentation.

In December 1967 a highway patrolman, Herb Schirmer, had a close encounter at Ashland, Nebraska. The aliens had told him they were undertaking a 'breeding analysis programme', but they did not go into details. On 3 May 1968 nineteen-year-old nurse's aide,

Shane Kurz, was abducted by a UFO. Afterwards, she found a red ring around her abdomen and stopped menstruating. A gynaecologist was baffled by her case and a hypnotist was called in. It was then discovered that the aliens had extracted ova from her, telling her that she had 'been chosen to have a baby for us'.

In October 1974, an entire family was abducted from their car on a quiet road in Essex. Inside the UFO were two types of being: tall humanoid entities that seemed to be in control and small squat Greys that conducted medical tests – an all too familiar aspect of these abductions. However, in this case, the family was also given a tour of the craft and shown a series of films. These told of the aliens' genetically barren home world. The aliens said that they had come to Earth to ensure we did not go the same way as they had done, explaining: 'You are our children. You are part of an experiment.'

Meanwhile, in Rawlins, Wyoming, in 1974, a hunter was abducted – only to be rejected by the aliens because he had had a vasectomy. Elsie Oakensen was abducted by a dumb-bell-shaped UFO near Church Stowe in Northamptonshire, only to be rejected because she was too old. She was given healing powers as a consolation prize. The aliens then abducted three young women from nearby Preston Capes. And on 15 October 1979, a postmenopausal concert pianist, Luli Oswald, was abducted while driving down a coastal road in Brazil. She was given a gynaecological examination, but rejected. However, her companion, a twenty-five-year-old student, was accepted into the alien programme.

In 1980, aliens removed eggs from a Finnish abductee's ovaries using a long tube. Again she was told her that their race was genetically sterile, but that they had found within humanity an unexpectedly rich gene pool. This was helping them keep their species alive.

Female abductees often find themselves pregnant after an encounter. One Lancashire woman was shocked to find herself pregnant – she did not even have a boyfriend at the time. However, she had been abducted a few days before and gynaecologically examined by a female alien. After a few weeks, she miscarried, losing a large amount of blood. By then she was convinced the aliens had impregnated her, then taken the foetus which continued its development elsewhere.

In a study of fifty British abduction cases, it was found that four women became unexpectedly pregnant immediately after their encounter, then had a mysterious miscarriage within three months. One case involved a young woman called Karen. In 1979 she and her boyfriend had taken a holiday job in Cornwall. One night, Karen had a close encounter with a strange and blinding light. When she return home to Cheshire she found herself pregnant, but she was plagued with strange dreams. In them, she would have the baby, but it would have an odd appearance and preternatural intelligence. But three months into her pregnancy, Karen awoke to find her bed covered in blood. She was no longer pregnant, but instead of feeling bereft, because of the dreams, she felt relieved. This, in turn, brought on a terrible sense of guilt. But this was by no means the end of the matter. Karen went on to have a number of other strange encounters with UFOs and aliens. Then, in early 1987, she awoke in the middle of the night to find herself holding the hand of a small child. A ball of light rose upwards through the ceiling and the child vanished. It was a brief encounter, but it brought her comfort. She felt that the child she had lost to the aliens had returned briefly to show her that it had survived and was flourishing in some other realm.

There is some physical proof of the 'starchild' theory. It was unearthed in the 1930s, when a teenage American girl was taken by her parents to visit relatives in a small rural village about a hundred miles south-west of Chihuahua in northern Mexico. There were numerous caves and mine shafts in the area and, for her own safety, her parents told her not to go near them. But she was a teenager and a warning was not going to stop her.

One day, while exploring a disused mine shaft in the hills, she found a human skeleton lying on the ground. The skeleton's hand was holding a malformed skeletal hand that was sticking up out of the ground beside it. The girl scraped away the dirt to find a shallow grave. The malformed hand was attached to another complete skeleton. This was smaller than the first and terribly deformed.

As her parents had forbidden her to explore the caves and tunnels, she could hardly tell them about her find. But she took the two skulls and kept them for the rest of her life. When she died, they came into the possession of an American couple, who knew something of the story of their discovery. They had read researcher Lloyd Pye's book *Everything You Know Is Wrong – Book One: Human Origins* and, in February 1999, they went to see him to discuss the skulls. In particular, they wanted his opinion of the smaller of the two skulls which, although clearly humanoid, was like nothing they had ever seen before.

'I nearly fell from my chair when they handed it to me,' he said. 'It was precisely how I imaged a "Grey" skull might look, and I felt strongly from the first moment that it was at least partially alien.'

The couple hoped that Pye would arrange to have a scientific study performed on the skull to determine if it belonged to a poor, misshapen human child, or something else entirely. Pye was happy to oblige and began talking to various anthropologists, pathologists, dentists, ophthalmologists, paediatricians, radiologists and anyone else with specialised knowledge who might help.

The couple were not rich and Pye had no funding for the research but various experts in the field examined the skull as a favour. The larger skull had a confusing mixture of cranial features, but in general it looked more female than male. It had cheekbones that could belong to either sex. But it had the slender brow ridge of a female and it was small and light compared with human norms. All but one of the teeth, a rear molar, were present. The cusps of the teeth were worn flat, and the dentists guessed that it would require no less than twenty years of eating grit-laced food to cause such cusp wear. The consensus was that the skull belonged to a female in her late twenties.

The upper jaw had become detached from the other skull. Technically it could not be considered part of the other skull without expensive DNA matching, but it was of the right size and carried a similar pattern of staining. It seemed a sure bet that it did belong to the skull, though. It carried the only two teeth of the smaller skull. These were milk teeth and were about to be replaced by adult molars. It was concluded that the second skull belonged to a child of five or six years old.

However, not all the experts agreed. Some pointed to a cranial suture between the lower left parietal area and the upper left occipital bone on the left rear quadrant of the head. Here, there was a three-inch line of small 'islands' of bone. These grow to fill in gaps appearing in suture lines during periods of rapid, sustained growth – such as those that take place during adolescence. Those islands made the skull appear much older than five years – it could have belonged to a fifteen year old.

Pye then began to consider the details of how the skulls were found. Unfortunately, the girl who had first discovered the skeletons years before was not alive and could not be questioned. He was particularly interested in the malformation of the smaller skeleton, but there was no way that this could be determined. But details of how they had been found intrigued him. One skeleton being above the ground with its hand holding that of the buried skeleton led him to postulate that the two individuals had died in some kind of murder suicide pact, with the older one killing the younger one and burying it before taking her own life.

During his investigation, Pye discovered that there was a legend concerning 'Star Beings' throughout the whole of Latin America. This legend concerns extraterrestrials – types we now call Greys – who impregnate native women. The offspring would be allowed to stay with their mother until the age of six or so, then they would be repossessed by the aliens.

Pye realised that the 'Star Being' legend tied in perfectly with his murder–suicide scenario. Imagine a woman in her late twenties who had been impregnated by an alien. She gave birth and had raised the hybrid child to the age of around six, when the pick-up time was approaching. Then she somehow received word that the aliens were coming to retrieve her child. But she was not willing to give it up. Instead of letting the aliens take it away to some unknown fate, she took it into a mine shaft, killed it and buried it in a shallow grave, leaving one of its hands sticking up out of ground. Then she held onto her child's hand as she poisoned herself and lay down beside the child's body to die.

The woman concerned would have to be in some kind of state to do such a thing and Pye found evidence of a blow to the larger skull's left parietal bone above and to the rear of the left ear not long before death. This would have caused concussion, just the sort of brain-addling injury that might have caused a loving mother to put such a lethal scheme into action, he reckons.

During Pye's investigation, he was contacted by Mrs Karen Scheidt. She had a photograph of similar 'starchild' skulls, which she had taken while holidaying in Cholula, northern Mexico in 1975. The guide told her that the two skulls belonged to 'gods' that had come down from the sky centuries before to teach the local people astronomy, mathematics and how to live in harmony with nature. These gods were planning to return to their home in the heavens. Before they could do so, another bunch of gods turned up. There was an almighty battle and the two gods were killed. They were buried in a small shrine near the main temple at Cholula, which became a place of pilgrimage for the local people.

New Religion

So is the modern-day belief in UFOs really a new religion that mirrors the needs and beliefs of those who live in the new scientific age? Certainly people had seen things flying around in the sky before 1947 when Kenneth Arnold inadvertently dubbed them 'flying saucers'. Indeed, Christ was seen to ascend into the sky after his 'death' on the cross.

Consider this for an alien encounter. At a time of great upheaval

During 1917 local children saw visions of the Virgin Mary at Fatima, Portugal, and the crowds gathered. On 13 October they witnessed a miracle as the sun danced in the sky. Here people watch the solar phenomena.

in the world, a humanoid being appeared to three witnesses and announces that it is 'from above'. For the next six months, they have traumatic visions. When the being leaves, an estimated 50,000 to 70,000 people see what they called the 'Dance of the Sun'. The shining disc descends through the clouds, spins and dives towards the Earth in a flash of light and heat. This would normally be considered a first class alien encounter report. Only it is the story of the so-called 'visions at Fatima' where the Virgin Mary appeared to three young girls in Portugal in 1917.

In ancient times all heavenly objects had a religious significance – whether they came from God or Satan. However, with the retreat of religion at the end of the nineteenth century, few admitted to seeing flying angels. Objects seen in the skies were just one of many mysteries that were subsequently called 'Fortean', after writer and investigator Charles Fort (1874–1932). Fortean investigators simply referred to such anomalous bodies as 'objects seen floating'. But, after Kenneth Arnold, flying saucers acquired a status of their own.

Charles Fort (1874-1932), photographed around 1920.

The explosion of interest in UFOs and the mythologies that surround them have led many to compare it to the founding of a new religion. UFOs and their alien occupants live in a sphere far higher than that occupied by mere terrestrials. Although Kenneth Arnold reported his sighting because he believed that what he had witnessed might be Soviet military hardware, the idea that anomalous objects and lights in the sky were aliens visiting from outer space caught on very quickly.

Because of the birth of aerial bombings, the development of ballistic missiles and the dropping of the atomic bomb, people naturally had their eyes on the skies. These unprecedented technological advances also spawned the idea that there was a great deal more in the scientific world that we did not understand. But maybe, there was someone out there who did. Certainly the impossible manoeuvrings of UFOs suggested that there was.

It was some time before reports of the 'beings' that pilot flying saucers emerged. UFO research groups tried to suppress the accounts of contactees. However, when they did speak out about their encounters it seemed that the aliens had a message for us. George Adamski encountered an alien 1952, who warned him that Earth must learn to control its use of nuclear energy. Coincidentally, Adamski met his 'Venusian' just three weeks after America exploded the first hydrogen bomb.

Adamski made no secret of the religious dimension of his testimony. Many saw him as a modern-day prophet. He was an emissary of some heavenly force bringing higher wisdom to humanity whose folly risked bringing down the apocalypse. It is not difficult to see how such ideas could have taken hold.

From the beginnings of the scientific revolution in the West, a belief system based on religion had been replaced by scientific reason and logic. In 1843, John Stuart Mill published *A System of Logic*, which was closely followed by Charles Darwin's *On The Origin of Species* in 1858. These writings undermined organised religion. With other works, they set out 'the scientific principle', which rejected as 'unreal' anything that was not amenable to reason or scientific experiment.

Science brought with it tangible benefits – the automobile, electric light, the aeroplane, everything that was modern and new. It also brought with it the mechanised slaughter of the First and Second World Wars. By the 1950s, the dream of science was becoming a little tarnished. The shadow of the 'Bomb' that hung over world affairs brought widespread disillusionment with the very real achievements of science. Scientists were portrayed as 'Frankensteins' who had created the monster that would destroy civilisation, humankind and the planet. However this did not halt the decline of the old religions. What was needed was something new.

It was into this world that Erich von Däniken launched his book *Chariots of the Gods*. The book contained the radical proposition that humanity had, in the past, been seeded by extraterrestrials whom our ancestors later mistook for gods. The book became an instant bestseller and turned von Däniken into a world-wide celebrity. He had hit the mood of the moment, and his later books became enormously influential.

His book emerged at a time when many were desperate for something to believe in. The old religions had been largely discredited by science, and science itself was tainted. What von Däniken did was give his readers the best of both worlds. His 'gods' were tangible and real and, if you will, scientific. They brought to Earth the wisdom of the heavens. What's more, unlike the gods of the old religions, von Däniken's were, like scientific theories, open to testing. The existence of his 'gods' could be proved – if you proved that flying saucers existed.

Although science has set its face against UFOlogy, in the same way it attacked the old religions, the UFO phenomenon exists within the realm of science itself. Its extraterrestrial 'gods' are not metaphysical beings but scientists – only they are better than our terrestrial scientists because they can fly effortlessly among the stars.

Until cast-iron proof of the existence of alien visitors is produced, the idea of extraterrestrials should be considered a myth. But why do we need myths? They seem to be vital to human life. No culture we know of has ever existed that did not have a mythology. 'Myth is a dramatic shorthand record of such matters as invasions, migrations, dynastic changes, admission of foreign cults, and social reforms,' said scholar of mythology Robert Graves. In other words, myths are the metaphors through which we make sense of the world in which we live. So modern myths must encompass the awesome power of technology, a distrust of government, the need for wisdom and knowledge from a source that is untainted and the desire for salvation in a world where God has all but been destroyed. UFO mythology involves all of this. Not only are extraterrestrials more technologically advanced than we are, they are able to control technology in a way that we have yet to achieve. The fact that governments are deemed to be withholding UFO secrets speaks volumes about our alienation from the political process. Extraterrestrials bring wisdom and they offer us transportation into a higher realm. They fulfil the emotional and spiritual needs that science and rationalism have failed to provide for and have given us the gods back again, but this time, as scientifically acceptable gods. In *The Republic*, Plato pondered whether one myth could be constructed that would be believable and meaningful to the whole world. Perhaps that it what UFOs provide.

Heaven's Gate

The quasi-religious UFO theories of Marshall Applewhite, leader of the Heaven's Gate cult, had lethal consequences for his followers. His belief that a UFO was heading towards Earth in the wake of the Hale–Bopp comet to take his followers to the 'Next Level' led to the biggest mass suicide in North America.

It became clear that something was terribly wrong when, on 25 March 1997, Federal Express delivered a package of videocassettes to the San Diego, California, home of ex-cult member Richard Ford. The tapes were from Marshall Applewhite. When Ford played the cassettes, he found that they were essentially videotaped suicide notes, with cult members giving what they termed 'exit statements'. Ford showed his employer the tape and they went to the cult's headquarters at Rancho Santa Fe, a secluded mansion on the outskirts of San Diego. Inside, they found the bodies of thirty-nine cult members – eighteen men and twenty-one women – in various stages of decomposition. Death had been caused by a lethal cocktail of vodka and phenobarbitol, a powerful sedative.

There was no sign of rush or panic. It was plain the mass suicide had been rigorously planned. All the victims were dressed in the same dark outfits and wore new trainers. They had their hands by their sides and they were staring at the ceiling through a three-foot square of purple silk, folded into a triangle pointing downwards. Many of the corpses were neatly arranged in their beds, which suggested that the suicides had been carried out in shifts. Their bags were packed and they carried identification details in their shirt pockets. It seemed inexplicable that so many people had gone to their deaths without putting up a struggle.

Many more people – over nine hundred – had died at Jonestown but some had struggled and others escaped. The cult was facing a Congressional enquiry and, basically, the game was up for cult leader Jim Jones. More died at Waco, but the eighty-one Branch Davidians who perished there died during a shoot-out with the FBI. Some seventy members of the Solar Temple died believing that they would be reincarnated on Sirius if they died a fiery death on Earth. However, some were murdered by their leaders, who were under investigation for fraud. The Heaven's Gate deaths were different. They was no confrontation with the authorities and, seemingly, no coercion. Applewhite and his followers had gone peacefully into the arms of death.

They had made no secret of their plans. From 1993 onwards, Heaven's Gate had promoted itself as the 'last chance to advance beyond human'. They had taken advertisements in the national press and ran a website announcing their intention to leave this Earth. However, Applewhite promised his followers that they would taken aboard a UFO. For that reason, Heaven's Gate had been dubbed the 'UFO cult'.

Born in Spur, Texas on 17 May 1931, Applewhite was the son of a Presbyterian minister. He attended Austin College in Sherman, Texas, and it was thought that Applewhite would follow his father into the seminary. Instead, he decided to pursue a career in music. A talented singer, he took the lead in the college productions of *Oklahoma!* and *South Pacific*. He later sang at the Houston Grand Opera, then became music professor at a Catholic college in Houston. In the 1950s, he married and had two children and led a conventional life. Then a string of homosexual affairs over a period of three years at the end of the 1960s ruined his marriage, and he was sacked from his college post after a scandal involving the daughter of a trustee. In 1971 Applewhite booked himself into a mental hospital in Houston, Texas, and begged to be 'cured' of his homosexuality.

There, he met Bonnie 'Lu' Nettles, a psychiatric nurse who, like Applewhite, came from a deeply religious background. Nettles abandoned her family and she and Applewhite went on the road as

New Age gurus, while wandering around the US under a variety of names, including 'Brother Sun' and 'Sister Moon', 'Him' and 'Her', and 'Bo' and 'Peep'.

Applewhite and Nettles claimed to have been sent to Earth by a spaceship to teach humans how to attain a level beyond Earth. Together they set up a cult called Human Individual Metamorphosis (HIM) in California. Followers had to give up their names and their property and become celibate. However, HIM fell apart after various prophecies failed.

For a while, Applewhite and Nettles supported themselves by stealing cars and credit card fraud. Then in 1973, Applewhite had a revelation that they were the biblical 'Two Witnesses' who would rise from the dead before ascending to heaven in a cloud. A year later, the cloud became a UFO. By this time, Nettles and Applewhite, now referring to themselves as 'The Two', had begun to attract devotees and they organised them into a new UFO cult. They moved back to Texas, where Applewhite took out a full-page advertisement that invited people to join. The cult used the names Total Overcomers Anonymous and Higher Source. Those who responded were sent a video showing Applewhite and two zonked-out followers who appeared to hang on every word that issued from the guru's lips. As with all such cults, their philosophy centred around total acceptance of the leaders' ideas, no matter how bizarre.

Yet, far from alienating potential members, it was the cult's more extreme ideas concerning UFOs that actually drew in new recruits. Indeed, when, in the mid-1970s, this mythology was propounded in a series of public lectures, the result was to bolster the cult's membership and considerably increase its media profile.

UFO Magazine published a feature on the cult. In it, Applewhite referred to himself as Do and Nettles as Te. It is thought that these were taken from the notes played to signal the aliens in the film *Close Encounters of the Third Kind*. However, there may have been another influence. Do – who also called himself Father John Doe and even King Do – had a special affection for *The Sound of Music*. Te in that film was, like the poison the suicide cult took, a 'drink with jam and bread, which takes you back to Do'. Other cult members were called Re, So and Fah. This may sound ludicrous, but Applewhite was painfully serious. He and some of his senior lieutenants had themselves castrated so that they could more easily live up to Applewhite's requirement that they should be totally celibate.

With media interest came paranoia. 'The Two' were plagued by the fear of assassination and throughout the late 1970s and into the 1980s the group became a shadowy entity, adopting several different names and living in a series of camps across Arizona, California and Montana. This did nothing to dent Applewhite and Nettles' growing cult status and, in 1982, they were made the subject of a TV film entitled *The Mysterious Two*. Afterwards, Applewhite outlined his beliefs in a screenplay called *Beyond Human: Return of the Next Level*. The American TV network NBC expressed interest.

Nettles' death from cancer in 1985 was a blow. But Applewhite soon decided that she had merely left for the 'Next Level'. He then declared himself to be the 'expected Messiah'. The cult all but disappeared, only to resurface five years later in 1990 with a new name. The cult moved into a $1.3 million mansion in San Diego County which had once been the home of Douglas Fairbanks Jr. Set in three acres on a hilltop, the lavish retreat was leased to the cult by its owner Sam Koutchesfahani, a convict fraudster who had run a scam that involved bribing colleges to enrol students from the Middle East who had already entered the US illegally.

When the cult members moved in, they had no contact with their millionaire neighbours. They slept on bunk beds. They were not allowed to drink or smoke and they had to cut off all contact with their families. To earn money, they turned to the internet, designing websites. This was highly profitable. The mansion was packed with computers. Their own website advertised their wares.

'Higher Source is very much "in tune" with the current pulse and future direction of technology,' they boasted. What's more, their leaders 'had worked closely together for over twenty years. During those years each of us has developed a high degree of skill and know-how through personal discipline and concerted effort.

We try to stay positive in every circumstance and put the good of a project above any personal concerns or artistic egos. This crew-minded effort, combined with ingenuity and creativity, has helped us provide advanced solutions.'

The cult's website also preached Applewhite's paranoid concoction of UFO fantasies and apocalyptic Christianity. Anyone receiving one of Applewhite's e-mail sermons could not help but understand that, for Heaven's Gate, the 'End' was at hand. He made it clear that only by leaving their bodies behind could he and his followers join the ethereal spacecraft that would take them to the 'evolutionary level above human'. In 1996, over the Internet, the cult gave notice of its imminent departure to join the 'Next Level mothership'.

On the night of 22 July 1995, the comet Hale–Bopp had been discovered independently by amateur astronomer Thomas Bopp of Phoenix, Arizona, and Alan Hale, head of the Southwest Institute for Space Research in New Mexico. Then in November 1996, amateur astronomer Chuck Shramek announced on UFOlogist Art Bell's popular radio show that he had seen a strange, unidentified object, which seemed to be travelling alongside the approaching Hale–Bopp comet. Pictures were posted on the Net and prominent UFOlogists such as Whitley Strieber speculated that it might be an alien spaceship. It did not take long for Applewhite to decide that this was the long-awaited shuttle to the 'Next Level'.

Within months the comet was nearing its closest approach to Earth and cult members were finalising their plans to 'shed their containers' (bodies) and 'ascend to the Next Level'. In early March 1997 the cult's website declared their intentions clearly: 'Hale–Bopp's approach is the marker we've been waiting for,' it said. 'We are happily prepared to leave this world.'

One of the cult's clients was the San Diego Polo Club, which asked Higher Source to do some more work for them early the next year. They got an e-mail back saying that Higher Source could not do any work after that Easter, owing to a 'religious festival'.

Cult members wore badges saying they were the 'Heaven's Gate Away Team'. They were an 'away team' in the *Star Trek* sense – a group of crew members that has beamed down to the surface of a planet to visit alien life-forms there. Members thought of themselves as caterpillars. Their bodies were 'vehicles' or 'containers' they could leave behind. The comet Hale–Bopp was 'the sign we've been waiting for'. Following unseen behind it would be 'the spacecraft to take us home'.

Their departure was again announced on the Internet. 'RED ALERT – Hale–Bopp brings closure to Heaven's Gate,' their home page said. By way of explanation, Applewhite added: 'I am in the same position in today's society as the one that Jesus was in… If you want to go to Heaven, I can take you through that gate – it requires everything of you.' The approach of Hale–Bopp meant: 'Our twenty-two years of classroom here on planet Earth is finally coming to conclusion – "graduation" from the Human Evolutionary Level. We are happily prepared to leave "this world" and go with [the spaceship's] crew.'

The website also contained a warning: 'Planet about to be recycled – Your only chance to survive – Leave with us.'

The cult prepared for their departure by sending videos explaining what they were going to do to former cult members.

'By the time you get this we'll be gone – several dozen of us,' said a note accompanying the video that Richard Ford received. 'We came from the Level Above Human in distant space and we have now exited the bodies that we were wearing for our earthly task, to return to the world from whence we came – task completed.'

'We couldn't be happier about what we're about to do,' said one cult member on the video.

'Maybe they're crazy for all I know,' said a woman cultist. 'But I don't have any choice but to go for it, because I've been on this planet for thirty-one years and there's nothing here for me.'

Another female follower, who apparently believed – groundlessly – that Applewhite had terminal cancer, said: 'Once he is gone… there is nothing left here on the face of the Earth for me… no reason to stay a moment longer.'

All thirty-nine of the suicide victims appeared on the tape. They all had their hair cut short, leading the police to believe that they were all young men. In fact, their ages ranged from twenty-six to seventy-two and twenty-one of them were women.

In a second tape, Applewhite gave a long and rambling explanation of their beliefs.

'We came for the express purpose to offer a doorway to the Kingdom of Heaven at the end of this civilisation, the end of the millennium,' he said. 'Your only chance to evacuate is to leave with us. I guess we take the prize of being the cult of cults.'

The videos despatched, the thirty-nine members of the cult went out for a final meal in a local restaurant. They then split themselves into three groups and committed suicide in shifts over the next three days. Applewhite had kindly written out suicide instructions for each member: 'Take pudding or apple sauce and mix it with the medicine' – phenobarbitol – 'drink it down with a vodka mixture and relax.'

This was plainly ineffective. Most of the cult member died of suffocation and the last two suffocated themselves by putting plastic bags over their heads.

When Ford and his employer found the bodies, they called the police. The first two deputies who turned up were rushed to hospital. A Hazard Materials team was sent in to test for poisonous gases. The noxious fumes were discovered to have come from the victims' bodies. These were removed using a refrigerated lorry and a fork-lift truck.

With their containers disposed of by the San Diego Mortuary Department, the cult members' spirits reached the spaceship which took them home – well, no one can tell them that it didn't happen.

Afterwards, the police were on the alert for copycat suicides. Two more followers did indeed try to follow Applewhite in May 1997 even though, presumably, they had missed the ship. Acting on a tip-off from a CBS journalist, police went to a hotel some five miles from Rancho Santa Fe. There they found Wayne Cook from Las Vegas, apparently unconsious after taking an overdose. With him was Chuck Humphrey from Denver, also in a sorry state. Both were dressed in the regulation black with new trainers and had packed their bags for the trip. Purple shrouds to cover their faces were at hand. They had been members of the cult, but had left before the final send-off. They were rushed to hospital and both pulled through. They had survived, ironically, because they mis timed the despatch of their 'goodbye' videos.

Applewhite – 'Do' – left a chilling message for the world on the Internet, which remained there long after their deaths. It read:

Do's Intro: Purpose – Belief
What Our Purpose Is – The Simple 'Bottom Line'

Two thousand years ago, a crew of members of the Kingdom of Heaven who are responsible for nurturing 'gardens,' determined that a percentage of the human 'plants' of the present civilization of this Garden (Earth) had developed enough that some of those bodies might be ready to be used as 'containers' for soul deposits. Upon instruction, a member of the Kingdom of Heaven then left behind His body in that Next Level (similar to putting it in a closet, like a suit of clothes that doesn't need to be worn for awhile), came to Earth, and moved into (or incarnated into), an adult human body (or 'vehicle') that had been 'prepped' for this particular task. The body that was chosen was called Jesus. The member of the Kingdom of Heaven who was instructed to incarnate into that body did so at His 'Father's' (or Older Member's) instruction. He 'moved into' (or took over) that body when it was 29 or 30 years old, at the time referred to as its baptism by John the Baptist (the incarnating event was depicted as '...the Holy Spirit descended upon Him in bodily form like a dove' – Luke 3:22). [That body (named Jesus) was tagged in its formative period to be the receptacle of a Next Level Representative, and even just that 'tagging' gave that 'vehicle' some unique awareness of its coming purpose.]

The sole task that was given to this member from the Kingdom of Heaven was to offer the way leading to membership into the Kingdom of Heaven to those who recognized Him for who He was and chose to follow Him. 'The Kingdom of Heaven is at hand' meant – 'since I am here, and I am from that Kingdom, if you leave everything of this world and follow me, I can take you into my Father's Kingdom.' Only those individuals who had received a 'deposit' containing a soul's beginning had the capacity to believe or recognize the Kingdom of Heaven's Representative. They could get to His Father only through total reliance upon Him. He later sent His students out with the 'Good news of the Kingdom of Heaven is at hand,' and His followers could then help gather the 'flock' so that the 'Shepherd' might teach others what was required of them to enter His Father's House – His Father's Kingdom – the Kingdom of Heaven – in the literal and physical Heavens – certainly not among humans on Earth. Leaving behind this world included: family, sensuality, selfish desires, your human mind, and even your human body if it be required of you – all mammalian ways, thinking, and behavior. Since He had been through this metamorphic transition Himself from human to Level Above Human – under the guidance of His Father – He was qualified to take others through that same discipline and transition. Remember, the One who incarnated in Jesus was sent for one purpose only, to say, 'If you want to go to Heaven, I can take you through that gate – it requires everything of you.'

Our mission is exactly the same. I am in the same position to today's society as was the One that was in Jesus then. My being here now is actually a continuation of that last task as was promised, to those who were students 2000 years ago. They are here again, continuing in their own overcoming, while offering the same transition to others. Our only purpose is to offer the discipline and 'grafting' required of this transition into membership in My Father's House. My Father, my Older Member, came with me this time for the first half of this task to assist in the task because of its present difficulty.

Looking to us, and desiring to be a part of my Father's Kingdom, can offer to those with deposits that chance to connect with the Level Above Human, and begin that transition. Your separation from the world and reliance upon the Kingdom of Heaven through its Representatives can open to you the opportunity to become a new creature, one of the Next Evolutionary Level, rightfully belonging to the Kingdom of Heaven.

Why It Is Difficult To Believe or Accept Us

We don't know if you believe in the real existence of negative or 'lower' forces. If you do, then you may be able to understand or relate to some of what we are about to say. It seems that how your 'programming' permits you to see or identify those forces, determines the limit of your acceptance or understanding. Many believe that there are 'evil' acts or even 'evil' individuals, but would draw the line before they would believe in evil spirits, evil discarnates, negative influences, malevolent space aliens, 'Luciferians,' or Satan and his fallen angels.

The generally accepted 'norms' of today's societies – world over – are designed, established, and maintained by the individuals who were at one time 'students' of the Kingdom of Heaven – 'angels' in the making – who 'flunked out' of the classroom. Legends and scriptures refer to them as fallen angels. The current civilization's records use the name Satan or Lucifer to describe a single fallen angel and also to 'nickname' any 'evil presence.' If you have experienced some of what our 'classroom' requires of us, you would know that these 'presences' are real and that the Kingdom of God even permits them to 'attack' us in order for us to learn their tricks and how to stay above them or conquer them. The space aliens, or Luciferians, use the discarnate spirits (the minds that are disembodied at the death of a body) as their primary servants – against potential members of the Kingdom of God. These 'influences,' or discarnates, are constantly 'programming' every human 'plant' (vehicle or body), to accept a set of beliefs and norms for behavior during a lifetime. From our point of view, this 'programming' finds that body, and the vast majority of all human bodies, barely usable by students of the Kingdom of Heaven.

As the above example can serve to testify, the 'lower forces' would – through their 'norm' concept – what is 'socially acceptable,' what is politically correct – have you not believe in spirits, spirit possession, negative space aliens, Satan, etc. They would have you believe that to even dabble in these ideas is of the 'occult,' satanic, or at the least, giving credence to 'fringe' topics. That's where they would also categorize any mental search of

Eastern religions, astrology, metaphysics, paranormal, UFOs, etc., etc. In other words, they (these space aliens) don't want themselves 'found out,' so they condemn any exploration. They want you to be a perfect servant to society (THEIR society – of THEIR world) – to the 'acceptable establishment,' to humanity, and to false religious concepts. Part of that 'stay blinded' formula goes like this: 'Above all, be married, a good parent, a reasonable church goer, buy a house, pay your mortgage, pay your insurance, have a good line of credit, be socially committed, and graciously accept death with the hope that 'through His shed blood,' or some other equally worthless religious precept, you will go to Heaven after your death.'

Many segments of society, especially segments of the religious, think that they are not 'of the world,' but rather that their 'conversion' experience finds them 'outside of worldliness.' The next statement that we will make will be the 'Big Tester,' the one that the 'lower forces' would use to clearly have you discredit or disregard us. That statement is: Unless you are currently an active student or are attempting to become a student of the present Representative from the Kingdom of Heaven – you ARE STILL 'of the world,' having done no significant separation from worldliness, and you are still serving the opposition to the Kingdom of Heaven. This statement sounds – to humans who have been so carefully programmed by the 'lower forces' – arrogant, pompous, or egotistical at the least – as if by taking this stand we had something to gain – as if we were seeking recognition as 'Deity' or as self-appointed prophets.

That Luciferian programming has truly been effective, for we don't even want to voice to you the statement in question. However, believe it or not, it is only for your sake – the sake of prospective recipients of the Kingdom of Heaven – that we must 'tell the truth,' openly identify to you as Representatives of the Kingdom of Heaven, well aware of the 'fallout' of that position.

The hard facts or bold statements in a nutshell, that are so difficult to accept or 'digest' – come down to: If you want or ever expect to go to Heaven – here is your window. That window opportunity requires: 1) an incarnate (as human) Representative of the Kingdom of Heaven; 2) that all who hope to enter Heaven become active students of that Representative while the Representative is present; 3) those who endure the 'transition classroom' until it ends (adequately bonding or 'grafting' to that Representative) will go with that Representative – literally LEAVE the human kingdom and Earth as He is about to do. Staying behind, for any significant period, could jeopardize that 'graft.' That window to Heaven will not open again until another civilization is planted and has reached sufficient maturity (according to the judgement of the Next Level).

We can't blame you for 'buying into' the 'Luciferian' program. What else has been available during those periods when no Representative was present? Almost nothing – save some warnings in the Scriptures, i.e., Luke 20:34-36, Luke 21:23, Mark 12:25, and Mark 13:17-19. Check these out.

Another fact is that what someone is into during the time a Representative is not present really doesn't matter that much, except that they are found unprepared when One comes – the only time when the Kingdom of Heaven can be offered to you.

The dilemma is we are here and most humans are thoroughly 'hooked' to humanity. However, the same 'grace' that was available at the end of the Representative's mission 2000 years ago is available now with our presence. If you quickly choose to take these steps toward separating from the world, and look to us for help, you will see our Father's Kingdom.

It is clear to all of us, that to the Anti-Christ – those propagators of sustained faithfulness to mammalian humanism – we are, and will be seen as, their Anti-Christ. This is certainly to be expected, and it will not delay our return to our Father's Kingdom. It might even accelerate that return.

We will, between now and our departure, do everything we can for those who want to go with us. But we cannot allow them to interfere with or delay our return to Him.

The Present Representative

Do

If you are convinced by that and feel the urge to shed your container, remember that Heaven's Gate is closed. Hale–Bopp is on its way back out into the farthest corner of the solar system and it won't be coming back near Earth until 6210 – and you are going to be dead by then anyway.

In the aftermath of the suicides, the cult's history and the events leading up to the suicides were dissected minutely in an effort to understand what drove these people to take their own lives. Many commentators pointed to the strict regime Applewhite had imposed on his followers and claimed that the deaths, like those at Jonestown and Waco, were the result of powerful mind-control techniques by which followers became lost in the paranoid personality of their leader.

Others, however, focused on the UFO side of the story, claiming that the cult's destructive fantasies had been fuelled by figures in the UFO community suggesting that the unknown object said to be accompanying the Hale–Bopp comet might be an alien spacecraft. To many, the only difference between Heaven's Gate and other 'doomsday cults' was their choice of metaphor, with talk to UFOs and the 'Next Level' standing in for the more familiar sermons on Jesus, the Second Coming and the Kingdom of Heaven.

As it was, the comet Hale–Bopp had passed within a mere 156 million miles of Earth and could be seen plainly in the night sky. The object that Chuck Shramek said was accompanying it, and that some prominent UFOlogists speculated might be a spaceship, was never identified.

A Timeless Myth?

So are UFO and alien encounters really just modern-day fairy tales? There are certainly many parallels between folklore and modern alien encounters.

For example, in the 1857 book *Cumberland and Westmoreland Ancient and Modern,* author Jeremiah Sullivan recounts a tale, involving a man named Jack Wilson. One evening, when returning home, he noticed a ladder reaching down from a cloud and around the bottom of it was a large group of fairies. As he approached, the fairies spotted him and ran up the ladder. They drew it up after them, then 'shut the cloud' and disappeared.

These days we would not hesitate to dismiss such a fanciful tale. But there is no denying that it has strong parallels with the UFO encounter of patrolman Lonnie Zamora in New Mexico in 1964. Zamora saw an egg-shaped craft land in a desert gulch and two small aliens standing close by it. When the aliens spotted him they jumped back into her spacecraft and took off. The craft actually left physical evidence in the form of scorch marks.

UFOs: a Sighting by highway patrol officer Lonnie Zamora near Socorro, New Mexico, on 24 April 1964.

Those who do not believe in UFOs claim that what Zamora had actually seen was a plasma ball whose electromagnetic field induced a hallucination. The same thing could be true of the fairies seen by Jack Wilson. On the other hand, it could be that both witnesses actually encountered alien beings, but that their experiences were interpreted differently due to the prevailing ways of thinking of the time during which they took place.

Another powerful example of the similarity between folkfore and modern-UFO reports can be found in the Celtic traditions of Ireland. One of the central features of Celtic myth is a fabled supernatural realm. This is located within the Sidhs, or burial mounds, of the early people buried there. According to folklore, this other-world is a place of perfection where there is plenty of food and no illness or unpleasantness. The gods sometimes come into our world and invite mortals into their realm, though sometimes they take humans there by force. These are the Celtic equivalent of alien contacts and abductions. And occasional contactees and abductees are taken to a similar world of utopian perfection.

In her book, *Beyond the Light Barrier*, contactee Elisabeth Klarer reported how, in 1956, she had taken a flight in a flying saucer with an alien called Akon. They visited Akon's idyllic home-planet, Meton: a world free of war, politics and illness.

In Celtic tradition, once within such worlds, a mortal would experience time distortion. One minute spent there could be the equivalent of several years in the physical world and, similarly, years in the otherworld might pass in an instant of mortal time. Alien abductees regularly report the phenomenon of 'missing time'.

In his book *The Science of Fairy Tales*, Edwin S. Hartland relates the story of a Welshman who went to tend his cattle and came back three weeks later, thinking that he had only been gone three hours. During this period he said that he had been surrounded by little people who mesmerised him with their dancing and singing. Although these Welsh little people sound much nicer than their modern 'Grey' counterparts, many of the elements are otherwise the same as a modern-day alien abduction.

There is another bit of Celtic folklore that has a modern comparison. Fairy folk would often ask for pure water from their human contact. In return they would offer food, though it never contained salt. Compare that to the tale of Wisconsin farmer Joe Simonton, who saw a UFO land near his home in Eagle River in April 1961. When he went to check it out, he found an alien on board who appeared to be having a barbecue. He asked Simonton for some water. When he returned with it, the alien gave him a pancake. When it was analysed, it was found to contain no salt.

In ninth, century France a number of men were captured descending from an 'airship'. According to their captors they came from 'a certain region called Magonia, whence ships come in the clouds, and which bear away the fruits of the Earth to that same country'. Their captors asked Agobard, the bishop of Lyons, for permission to stone them to death. He refused as he did not believe the story.

The biblical tale of Noah and the ark is familiar in other guises around the world. In Mesopotamian mythology, the flood was planned by four gods. But a fifth, named Ea, told a man named Ut-Napishtin that he should build a boat and, like Noah, be saved. In 1997 Marshall Applewhite committed suicide along with thirty-eight of his followers because he thought the Earth was about to be recycled and a ship was coming to save then. Contactee

The dove sent from Noah's Ark. Engraving by Dore.

Marian Keech also marshalled her followers on the top of a hill, convinced that the Earth was about to be engulfed by a flood of biblical proportions and a flying saucer was on its way to save them. Sadly, her group broke up when neither saucer nor flood put in an appearance.

Legends of cloud ships with trailing anchors are also rife. In the tenth century it is said that a cloud ship's trailing anchor caught on the porchway of St Kinarus's church in Cloera, Ireland. One of the ship's occupants had to climb down and cut the rope, leaving the anchor behind. In March 1897, during a wave of phantom airship sightings seen across North America, Robert Hibbard claims to have been abducted when he was caught on a trailing anchor. It carried him for some distance before releasing him.

Another idea that has become central to UFOlogy is the idea that aliens are visiting Earth on a programme of genetic manipulation, designed to create human–alien hybrids. This idea also occurs in Greek mythology, where the god Zeus took several mortal women as his concubines and had children. With Niobe, for example, he had the hybrid son Argos.

Greek mythology has been particularly influential in Western culture and aspects are mirrored in the UFO phenomenon. The Greek location of the afterworld is a good example. In Homer's *The Odyssey*, the afterworld is said to be placed 'at the extremity of the Earth, beyond the vast Ocean'. At that time the River Ocean was thought to encompass the whole of the Earth. But later, when ships sailed the oceans and found more land beyond the horizon, the afterworld had to be relocated somewhere more distant and less accessible. It became the 'Kingdom of Shadows' and was placed at the centre of the Earth, where it could be reached only by the perilous journey into deep caverns, or by certain rivers that flowed down into the earth and on to the mystical realm.

The parallels here with the claims of the contactees are clear. In 1952, the home of the aliens who contacted George Adamski was Venus, still believed by some to be a paradise sister world of Earth. Since then probes have reached the planets and proved that it is one of the most inhospitable places in the solar system, and the location of the aliens' 'afterworld' has subsequently moved out of the solar system to planets orbiting distant stars or into other dimensions altogether.

In Greek myths, the gods often allowed some particularly noble or heroic individuals to break all the rules and inherit some godlike powers. This also happens in UFOlogy. Abductees often find they have been endowed with special powers after their abduction.

Of course, these parallels work both ways. While they can be used to argue that UFO and alien encounters are simply imagined to fulfil the human need for myths, they can also be used to demonstrate that aliens have been intimately involved with humans since the dawn of time.

Identified Flying Objects

So if UFOs are not alien spacecraft visiting Earth, what are they? Certainly some very funny things do go on in the atmosphere, not all of them are explainable, even by conventional science.

One case in point occurred at the beginning of June 1996, when a factory full of workers at a packaging factory in Tewkesbury in Gloucestershire, England, saw a ball of white light the size of a tennis ball burst through the roof of the factory and buzz erratically around the ceiling girders. Then the fizzing, sparking ball fell to the floor, giving the staff electric shocks and damaging equipment. Finally, it hit a window. Then the mysterious ball popped noisily like a soap bubble and vanished completely, leaving workers speechless.

But they were not the first to see the ball of light; shortly before the incident an aircraft passed through the heavy thunderclouds overhead and the crew had seen an anomalous ball of pure energy materialise as if out of nowhere next to the fuselage. It was this that fell to Earth and buzzed around the packaging works below.

But what exactly was this UFO? Perhaps it was one of the foo fighters that had been seen so often during World War II. Or was it something more mundane that had perhaps been overlooked by science?

The object in question was, it now appears, ball lightning. But for years, mainstream science had been saying that this meteorological phenomenon did not exist. However, dogged research on this fringe topic has produced an overwhelming weight of evidence – including photographs – that has finally forced science to accept that ball lightning is a real phenomenon.

This demonstrates just how blinkered scientific thinking can be. It also highlights that our knowledge of the skies is far from complete. It should be remembered that in 1770s the father of modern chemistry Antoine Lavoisier famously announced that meteorites were a myth. His reasoning was impeccable. In an address to the French Academy of Science in the 1770s, he pointed out that, as rocks did not live in the sky, they could not fall out of it. Despite the great man's wise words, meteorites do exist and the scientific community was eventually forced to accept the fact.

Today, meteorites and ball lightning are reported almost as commonly as flying saucers. However, it is generally assumed that over ninety per cent of UFO reports can be explained as the result of natural or technological occurrences. Consequently, it is assumed, quite falsely, that the other ten per cent can be explained that way too.

One of the first UFO debunkers to assume that there was a large degree of mistaken identity in UFO sightings was Dr Donald Menzel, the former Professor of Astrophysics at Harvard University. At the American Association for the Advancement of Science in 1969, Menzel presented his list of 'identified flying objects', claiming that they would eventually explain every flying saucers report.

Menzel divided his IFOs into categories:
- Material – aircraft, balloons, fireworks
- Immaterial – cloud formations, meteorological phenomena
- Astronomical – misidentified stars, planets, comets, meteorites
- Physiological – eye problems, after-images burned on to the retina
- Psychological – hallucinations, mass hysteria
- Photographic – double exposures, processing defects
- Radar anomalies

And then there were the hoaxes.

Admittedly, UFOlogy did need something of a more rigorous scientific approach at that time, but Menzel began to dismiss perfectly reliable UFO sightings by suggesting that the witnesses had actually seen spiders' webs, insects, soap bubbles or cigarette butts. As a result, his debunking backfired. It left UFO eyewitnesses looking more credible than the scientists debunking them. And, after a re-evaluation of many of Menzel's cases by Dr James McDonald, a former Director of the University of Arizona's Institute of Atmospheric Physics, many of Menzel's proposals were 'quantitatively absurd'. Even so, sceptics continue to go out of their way to find a rational explanation, even if none exists.

Take the classic case of RAF Intelligence Officer J.B.W. 'Angus' Brooks. In 1967, while walking his dog across Moigne Downs in Dorset, Brooks saw a long, thin, almost translucent craft flying towards him. As the object neared him, two more pieces of fuselage emerged from its side. They formed a perfect cross, roughly 170 feet wide, which then climbed into the morning sky and vanished.

Brooks was a trained RAF observer who had witnessed a UFO that could not have been mistaken for any conventional aircraft. It was less than three hundred yards away, in good light, just before midday. His credentials and experience could not have been bettered. But Ministry of Defence investigators and RAF psychologists decided that all he had seen were dead cells floating in the vitreous humour of his eyes.

Close Encounters of the Cinematic Kind

There was no implicit connection between the objects Kenneth Arnold saw in flight over Washington State in 1947 and the idea of aliens from outer space. Yet, in no time, the idea that flying saucers flown by extraterrestrials were visiting Earth was widespread. Some claim that the popular culture of the time was already set up to accept the reality of aliens.

From the beginning of the twentieth century, science-fiction writers had toyed with the notion of extraterrestrial races, and by the 1920s, there were numerous comic books and magazines pumping out wild ideas on the form extraterrestrial life might take. In 1936, aliens had made their celluloid debut in the series *Flash Gordon*, which created a cult following around the world.

But Arnold's sighting itself was the inspiration for a rash of science-fiction movies depicting alien invaders. They invariably came in saucer-shaped craft. Even in the 1953 movie *War of the Worlds*, the Martians attacked Earth in saucers – though, of course, H.G. Wells published the book in 1898.

Undoubtedly, eyewitness reports such as Arnold's have influenced the movies. But then movies have also influenced eyewitness reports. In the influential 1951 movie *The Day the Earth Stood Still*, a humanoid alien named Klaatu and his giant 'policeman' robot Gort arrive on Earth in a saucer-shaped spacecraft to warn humanity not to stray into outer space until it has cleaned up its nuclear act – a message often echoed by contactees and abductees. However, even some of the film's minor details would later find echoes in real-life accounts of alien contact. For example, Klaatu's silver suit clearly came from the same tailor as the one worn by the Venusian that George Adamski encountered the year after the film's release.

What's more, the interior of Klaatu's ship was strikingly similar to the description given a decade later by abductees Betty and Barney Hill. It came complete with platform beds for the medical examinations that have become a staple of the abduction phenomenon ever since.

In the 1953 movie *Invaders from Mars*, the aliens hid in secret underground bases, as they did in the 1955 movie *This Island Earth*. By the 1980s the notion of underground installations containing extraterrestrials and their technology lying beneath Area 51 in Nevada and the town of Dulce in New Mexico was widely accepted among UFOlogists.

Many of these early films also portrayed the extraterrestrials as hostile, emotionless and robot-like. Typical are the aliens that can adopt human form at will in the 1953 movie *It Came from Outer Space*, and the human replicants that grow in pods in *Invasion of the Body Snatchers* in 1956. The abductees still talk of their abductors as cold, emotionless automatons.

After the glut of science-fiction movies of the 1950s, there was a lull in the 1960s. But, interestingly, UFO sightings and alien encounters did not go away. So by the 1970s, a new generation of moviemakers had numerous new accounts of alien encounters to call on. Science fiction gave way to fact with full-on reconstructions of the accounts of prominent UFO eyewitnesses. *Hangar 18* told the story of the crash retrievals, while the story of Betty and Barney Hill's abduction was told in *The UFO Incident*.

In 1962, the year after the Hill's abduction, the TV puppet series *Fireball XL5* featured Grey aliens with large bald heads in an episode called 'Robert to the Rescue'. These aliens could take over a human's will and switch off their memory – just like the creatures the Hills had encountered.

In 1977, the UFO movie went big budget with *Close Encounters of the Third Kind*. This drew on numerous accounts from UFO eye-witnesses, contactees and abductees and wove them together into one storyline, then added the latest in special effects to bring the subject to a much wider audience than ever before. There were 550 more UFO sightings reported in the year following the movie's release than in the previous twelve months.

Soon a lot of details of *Close Encounters* began turning up in UFO and alien encounter reports. Naturally, Hollywood had pushed things over the top. The budget for the encounter at the climax of the movie stretched to a truly massive spacecraft, a first for Hollywood. After that, the spacecraft seen by UFO eyewitnesses got noticeably bigger. In one case, the pilot of flight JAL 1628 reported seeing a walnut-shaped object over Alaska, twice the size of an aircraft carrier.

Interestingly, although for years *ET*, released in 1982, was the top grossing movie of all time, it prompted no rash of similar sightings.

Hybrids have found their way into *Star Trek*, first with Mr Spock, the half-human and half-Vulcan, while in *Star Trek – The Next Generation*, Counsellor Troi is half-human, half-Betazoid, and Tasha Yar comes back after her death, through a complicated time-travel story, as half-human, half-Romulan. Meanwhile, back on Earth, there are people who claim to be the progeny of a one-night stand between an alien and a human.

Star Trek – The Next Generation also features a Holodeck, an artificial environment where real people undergo experiences that they can barely distinguish from the real thing. In the UFO literature this has several eerie forerunners. On the night of 30 May 1974, two people were driving towards Beit Bridge on the border of South Africa and what was then Rhodesia (now Zimbabwe). They spotted a UFO that kept pace with their car. Then they realised that they did not recognise the landscape round them. The road was straight, when it should have been windy. When they arrived at Beit Bridge, they discovered that they had used no petrol – when the journey should have used at least half a tank. Nor did the tyres show any wear. The two concluded that they had been transported to Beit Bridge on board the UFO in a room especially constructed to look like the real environment.

The movies and UFO reality intersected again in 1996, when the film *Independence Day* was launched on the 'ET Highway' outside Area 51 in Nevada. Many believed that it would smooth the way for the US government to reveal what it knew about the alien technology there. It was not forthcoming. Nevertheless, audiences across America rose cheering to their feet when the White House got zapped in the movie.

Plainly there is some kind of 'feedback loop' between science fiction and UFOlogy. Some have used this to suggest that all UFO accounts are fictitious, and simply inspired by what people see in the movies, while others claim that it is the real-life experiences of UFO eyewitnesses and abductees that are finding their way onto the silver screen.

The Hollow Earth

One of the wackiest theories in UFOlogy is that of the 'hollow Earth'. It's proponents point out that any environment that could support intelligent life is so far from Earth that meeting an extra-terrestrial is about as likely as meeting Elvis in the local supermarket. Consequently, aliens must come from somewhere closer to home. And there is only one place that their home could be – beneath our very feet.

Hollow-Earth theorists maintain that there is a world within our world, where an environment exists not very different from our own. It has its own inner landscape and its own life forms that have evolved separately from those on the outside. Its higher creatures are more advanced than we are, and they are the aliens we see visiting our outer world.

The idea that the Earth is hollow is not a recent invention. Myths that an underworld exists stretch back to the dawn of time. Usually it is the home of the souls of the damned, demons, trolls, elves and other supernatural beings.

However, in 1692, astronomer Edmond Halley speculated that within the Earth there is another concentric innermost sphere. A luminous atmosphere provides light to this inner world and allows creatures to live there. The aurora, or northern lights, that we see are in fact, some of the luminous gases escaping from the interior, Halley said.

In 1812 former US army officer John Cleves Symmes began a lecture tour of America, setting out his theory that the Earth is made up of five spheres, one within the other. He said that it was habitable within, and that the oceans, flowed in and out of openings at the poles. His ideas were popularised in the 1820 novel called *Symzonia* by Adam Seaborn, which may have been a pseudonym adopted by Symmes. He pledged to explore this new inner world and, in January 1823, he petitioned Congress, requesting that the government organise an expedition to claim the lands of the Earth's interior for the United States. But sadly

The planetary spheres. from Cunninghams *CosmographicallGlasse*,1559.

Congress refused to fund this harebrained scheme, and Symmes died in 1829 without putting his theory to the test.

But the hollow-Earth theory did not die with Symmes. After his death a full exposition of his theories was give in *The Symmes Theory of Concentric Spheres, Demonstrating that the Earth is Hollow, Habitable Within, and Widely Open About the Pole*, written by one of his sons. Although the scientific community refused to take the idea seriously, it may have prompted America's exploration of the polar regions between 1838 and 1842.

Cyrus Teed then came up with an even more bizarre hollow-Earth theory. He claimed that we were actually living on the inside of a hollow sphere – just 750 miles in diameter and 25,000 in circumference – which contained everything in the visible universe. The Moon, he said, was around half-a-mile across, while the Sun was less than three feet in diameter. The light curved in such a way

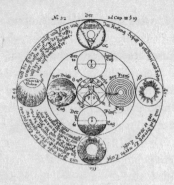

A model of the microcosmic man according to the Christian cabbalistic system.

to make them look bigger. This bending made it look like the Earth fell away from us, so that we could only see part of it. It also made part of the central region invisible and celestial bodies were seen to set and rise by passing by in and out of this region. The idea was, of course, a religious one. Instead of the Earth being an insignificant rock in a vast universe, it became all there is. Teed changed his name to Koresh (note the similarities with the Waco incident) and, with his followers, established a community of believers at Koreshanity in Florida.

Jules Verne published *Le Voyage au centre de la Terre* in 1864, which was translated into English as *A Journey to the Centre of the Earth* in 1874. Then in 1906, William Reed published *Phantom of the Poles,* in which he predicted that the interior of the hollow Earth could 'be made accessible to mankind with one-fourth the outlay of money, time and life that it cost to build the subway in New York City.' However, in 1909 Robert Perry reached the North Pole and two years later Roald Amundsen reached the South Pole – and neither reporting seeing any giant openings there.

Undeterred, hollow-Earth theorists re-evaluated their position, and in 1913, Marshall B. Gardner published *A Journey to the Earth's Interior, or, Have the Poles Really Been Discovered?* In it, he dismissed Symmes' fanciful idea that there were five concentric spheres within the Earth. According to Gardner, the Earth was simply hollow, warmed by an inner sun some six hundred miles in diameter. There were openings at the poles, however, which were over a thousand miles across. Speculation was rife about what sort of creatures lived down there.

The theory suffered another setback with Richard E. Byrd's flights over the North Pole in 1926 and over the South Pole in

1929. On these flights, no openings were seen. Still, the hollow-Earth theory was far from dead.

In a 1945 issue of *Amazing Stories* Ray Palmer published the tales of a fictional character named Richard Shaver, who described the activities of a race of subterranean beings called the Deros. And in 1957 Palmer launched a new pulp magazine, *Flying Saucers from Other Worlds*, in which he claimed that flying saucers originated in the interior of the Earth.

Since then every inch of the Arctic and Antarctic have been flown over, and the whole of the Earth has been surveyed by satellites. But the hollow-Earth theorists would still not give up. In June 1970 Palmer printed of a satellite photograph that showed a dark hole around the north pole.

The photograph was taken by the satellite ESSA-7 on 23 November 1968. It showed the whole of the northern hemisphere bathed in sunlight with a dark circular region centred on the pole in the middle. The accompanying story said: 'Although, surrounding the polar area, and north of such areas as the North American continent and Greenland and the Asian continent, we can see the ice-field – eight-foot thick ice – we do not see any ice fields in the large circular area directly at the geographic pole. Instead we see a hole.'

The picture was genuine. However, it was not a snapshot. It was a picture compiled throughout the day, so all the continents are shown in daylight, while the dark 'hole' in the centre was the region in perpetual polar winter night.

Undaunted, in 1979 Raymond Bernard published *The Hollow Earth: The Greatest Geographical Discovery in History*. According to Bernard, the Earth is a hollow shell eight hundred miles thick. The inner surface is illuminated by an inner sun six hundred miles in diameter. The aurorae are its reflection in the clouds.

Seismic data demonstrate clearly that the Earth is not hollow. However, Bernard also claims that other celestial bodies are also hollow. He says that the bright polar regions of Mars, thought by scientists to be ice caps, are the light of the planet's inner sun shining out. This cannot be disproven, though it is thought unlikely.

And still, the hollow-Earthers cling on tenaciously. They say that the polar openings are being concealed by the advanced technology of the inner-Earth dwellers. Indeed, the openings are not three-dimensional ones but exist in some higher dimension. In 1995 a hollow-Earther corresponding with an Internet discussion group wrote: 'The Earth is hollow in the fourth dimension... There are two "entrances", and these are reflected in the physical world as the north and south magnetic poles.'

Hollow-Earth theorists point out that explorers have reported that north winds get warmer nearer the poles, suggesting that they are warmed by air emanating from the Earth's interior. They also say that tropical plants have been found in the melt-waters of icebergs. Surely this misplaced flora came from within the Earth.

There is, of course, a government cover-up concerning the hollow Earth. American polar flyer Richard E. Byrd did, in fact, discover the polar openings, but was forced to pretend otherwise. A document that purports to be Byrd's diary was made public by his grandson and appeared on the Internet. It is dated 1947; Byrd went to the Arctic in 1947 to search for sources of uranium ore. According to the 'diary', Byrd took off from his Arctic base on 19 February. After three hours of normal flight the magnetic and gyro compasses went crazy. After another hour, he was flying over a valley with lush green vegetation and saw a mammoth on the ground. Later, his controls went dead. His plane was taken over by disc-shaped craft with swastika markings, which escorted him to the ground.

Byrd was taken by German-speaking Nordics to meet one of their leaders in a crystalline city. This, he was told, was 'the domain of the Arianni, the Inner World of the Earth'. A great storm was coming to ravage the world, Byrd was told. But he was not to worry. A new world run by the inner-Earth beings would emerge from the ruins of the human race. Byrd told the Pentagon all he had learned but was ordered to remain silent. As a naval officer, he did what he was told.

Visits from a Higher Dimension

One of the theories that has become popular among UFOlogists is that UFOs are visitors from 'other dimensions'. This theory acknowledges the idea of the existence of 'alternate realities' – which would explain not just UFOs, but many other paranormal phenomena. Although these ideas seem as if they have been plucked from the furthest reaches of science fiction, they are actually under serious consideration by the world's leading theoretical physicists.

To some UFOlogists, the idea that UFOs exist in other, higher dimensions would explain their elusiveness. If an object did exist in a dimension beyond our ordinary realm of space and time, when it did show up in our dimensions, it would appear very alien indeed.

Imagine, for example, that you saw a shape appear from thin air, hanging there in space. Before your very eyes it grows larger, rotates slowly, then shrinks and vanishes without a trace. You would naturally call your local UFO society and report that you have seen an extraterrestrial craft. And they would file your sighting with thousands of similar reports they have collected over the past fifty years. But what you have just visualised is what would happen if a four-dimensional object passed through our three-dimension world. At any one moment you would merely be glimpsing a cross-section through a reality that you could not possibly visualise as a whole.

The idea that we live in three-dimensional space has been around since 300 BC, when the Greek mathematician Euclid wrote his famous textbook on geometry, *Elements*. However, in the early part of the twentieth century, Albert Einstein realised that some of the anomalous properties of electromagnetic radiation and gravity could be explained if we lived in four-dimensional space–time. He and German mathematician Hermann Weyl began to develop the idea that space and time were combined in a single, four-dimensional 'continuum'. The idea of this 'space–time continuum' is widely accepted in the world of science. However, the idea that there may be other dimensions is now a topic of hot debate in scientific circles.

It is very difficult for us to think in higher dimensions. However, Edwin A. Abbott came up with a useful analogy in his 1884 novel *Flatland*. In the book, the inhabitants of Flatland are squares, lines, angles and pentagons that are confined to a world that has just two dimensions. They are extremely thin and can move in any direction across the surface, but they have no concept of the third dimension of space that exists at right angles to their world. The book describes what happens when three-dimensional objects pass through their flat world. To us, who are used to living in a three-dimensional world, everything that happens seems ordinary and readily understandable, but for Flatlanders it seems spooky and mysterious.

For example, if a sphere passes through Flatland, it appears first as a single point that appears out of nowhere. This is where the surface of the sphere touches the plane of the flat world. As it passes through, Flatlanders would see the point turn into a circle this is the sphere's cross-section. It would grow slowly and reach a maximum size when the sphere is halfway through. Then it would shrink back down to a point before disappearing again.

So three-dimensional objects passing through a two-dimensional world appear to perform impossible tricks, just as UFOs seem to when they appear and disappear, change shape and perform impossible manoeuvres in our world.

To many UFOlogists, the idea that UFOs are glimpses of things that exist in higher dimensions is a good deal more credible than the extraterrestrial hypothesis. Even our cursory exploration of our own solar system has pretty much ruled out our neighbouring planets as a home for intelligent life. And if extraterrestrials lived on the planets of other stars, they would be faced with travelling impossible distances to visit us. But if UFOs existed in other dimensions, they would not have to inhabit a planet in our solar system. Nor would they have to tear holes in the fabric of space–time to get her of the universe. They could exist right here with us, but in a dimension that is normally imperceptible to us. The appearance of a UFO would then be the intersection of a higher dimensional object with our three dimensions of space. And when it left those dimensions, it would disappear.

There are problems here though. The main scientific theory to deal with other dimensions is known as 'string theory'. According to string theory, when the universe was born in the Big Bang, some 15 billion years ago, it had not four, but ten or eleven dimensions – scientists can't make up their minds. But as the universe expanded, three space dimensions and one dimension of time 'unrolled' and grew to their present vast extent, while the other dimensions remained 'rolled up'. They are so tiny that they play virtually no role on the scale of the universe as we know it. Unfortunately, this has little to offer the world of UFOlogy.

What Do They Want?

For over fifty years now UFOs have been visiting the Earth. Aliens have been seen around the globe. So what have they come for? Are they concerned space brothers who want to save us from ourselves? Are they evil aliens planning to conquer Earth and wipe out humankind? Or is it just our genetic material they are after?

In trying to work out exactly what the alien agenda is, researchers have come up with a bewildering array of theories. The task is complicated by the wide variety of aliens reported, ranging from different types of biological extraterrestrials to non-physical entities referred to as 'ultraterrestrials'. Then we have the problem of seeing things through exclusively human eyes, which define alien behaviour as benevolent or malevolent and slot everything into a convenient moral framework. This is no small matter. As we are on the threshold of developing technologies that will take us to the stars, the question of who is out there and what they want with us is becoming increasingly important. The information we have on the alien agenda comes from two main sources. One is observation of the activities of extraterrestials when they interact with Earth and its population. The other is from direct contact with extraterrestial intelligence, from what they do and what they say.

In the early days of UFO visits it was generally assumed that extraterrestials were necessarily hostile. Early UFO sightings often involved pilots or military personnel. They were trained to see any uninvited intrusion into a nation's air space as an act of hostility. UFOs were pursued and often fired on by intercept aircraft. There is some evidence to suggest that the real motive behind building particle beam weapons for use in the Strategic Defense Initiative was not simply to protect the West from Soviet missiles, but to fire at alien spacecraft. That equally applies to the new National Missile Defense system. In his book *UFOs: The Secret History,* German researcher Michael Hesemann describes how two spacecraft were shot down by Brookhaven National Laboratory on Long Island using SDI weaponry in 1989 and 1992.

However, although there are numerous reports of the military attacking alien craft, there are very few examples of the aliens responding in anything but a defensive mode. This alone suggests that they are tolerant and non-threatening.

They may be here merely to observe and even guide us. The UFO archives are crammed with reports of alien craft monitoring human technology – space shots, military bases, nuclear installations and missile silos. Documents released under America's Freedom of Information Act revealed that, in the 1970s, a number of Intercontinental Ballistic Missile sites were visited by UFOs. Again the aliens showed no hostile intent. Instead the missiles' seven-digit launch codes were scrambled, rendering the system harmless. As the aliens did not use America's defencelessness as an opportunity to attack, one can only assume that they were trying to protect us from our own self-destructive drives.

There has also been some direct intervention with human space technology, which shows that the extraterrestrials want to curtail certain human activities in space. In his book *Alien Agenda,* Jim Marrs shows that the aliens are imposing a selective space quarantine on us. They sabotage certain military payloads and disable probes that may discover alien bases throughout solar system. Marrs cites the loss of both Russian and American Martian probes. The Russian *Phobos 2,* he points out, photographed a disc-shaped object gaining on it just before it malfunctioned. According to Marrs, the US Army has trained teams of remote viewers who use their psychic abilities to examine distant events and objects. They have described small multifaceted objects in the upper atmosphere that are responsible for numerous set-backs in space launches, including the 1993 Titan and 1996 Mars rocket launches.

But if the alien agenda is largely benevolent, how does alien abduction fit into that pattern? Veteran UFO researcher David Jacobs insists that abductions are a fundamental violation of human free will and are a prime example of one highly advanced species exploiting another. But Dr John Mack disagrees. He sees abduction as a form of benevolent biological intervention. Extraterrestrials are creating a hybrid species to preserve human DNA because humankind faces extinction by our wilful destruction of the environment, he says.

'Evidently, what we have been doing to the Earth has not gone "unnoticed" at a higher, cosmic level,' he writes in his book *Passport to the Cosmos*. 'Some sort of odd intervention seems to be occurring here. We are not, apparently, being permitted to continue our destructive ways without some kind of "feedback".'

Dr Joe Lewells concurs, but sees the alien intervention as part of a larger pattern. In his book *The God Hypothesis* he recounts the tale of an abductee called Rebecca Grant. She maintained contact with insectoid extraterrestials who told her why extraterrestrials would not intervene directly to prevent human destruction of the environment. 'If ETs were to repair the Earth without making any changes in our behaviour, we would simply undo all the good they had done,' she said. 'We might survive long enough to find an even grander way to destroy ourselves, one that could harm worlds other than our own. These beings feel that, by saving the human race, they would be condemning themselves to a violent confrontation with us in the future.'

Grant said that several groups of extraterrestrial were trying to stimulate a higher consciousness in the form of psychic abilities and paranormal powers in abductees. Numerous abductees have discovered undreamed of physic abilities after an encounter. Brazilian abductee Vera Rubia is a good example of this. After encountering humanoid extraterrestrials in her home in the town of Valencia, she was able to diagnose a person's illness simply by thinking about them. Doctors who investigated her abilities found her to be accurate ninety-nine per cent of the time.

Aliens also give abductees lectures on the environment and the dangers of destroying it. Carlos Dias, abducted in Ajusco Park near Mexico City in 1981, said that the aliens impressed on him the interconnectedness of things.

'All the things I saw made me realise about the interaction between the smallest particle and the biggest,' he said. 'Each has a specific duty.' His abduction triggered in him a profound reverence for life, a need to get involved in conservation and a renewed wish to 'enjoy a beautiful living planet'.

If the information given to abductees by extraterrestrials is taken at face value, humankind seems to have reached a crisis point in its evolution. It is at a dangerous point of transition where our activity is becoming a cause of concern to a wide range of extraterrestrial civilisations. They are worried what we may do to ourselves and presumably, the galaxy around us. But, by and large, they are here to help.

This is also the conclusion of Dr Steven Greer, the director of the Center for the Study of Extraterrestrial Intelligences. His comprehensive survey of documents and case studies has led him write a list of the aliens' principal activities. These are:

- General reconnaissance of the Earth and its civilisations.
- Observation and assessment of our military and nuclear capabilities.
- Studying human psychology.
- Assessment of human development.
- Assessment of human technology.
- Monitoring the space programme, with particular interest in parts directed towards establishing colonies in space.
- Limited interaction with humankind to pass on information about themselves and accustom us to their presence.

Greer believes that all the aliens' aims are entirely benevolent, especially when you consider how much more technologically advanced they are. They regard us with the compassion a mature species would reserve for a fledgling one and are trying to guide us through this difficult stage in our development.

The Nightmare Begins

But what happens if the aliens really are hostile? There are still those who suggest that it is only a matter of time before the Earth is visited by an alien aggressor. Surely the aliens have been observing the Earth for over fifty years in preparation for just such an invasion. So what are the chances of survival for the human race? Unfortunately, the prognosis is bad – very bad.

While we know very little about the aliens, they know a great deal about us. SETI –the Search for Extraterrestrial Intelligence – is beaming out messages into the sky. They tell anyone out there who cares to listen the position of our solar system in the galaxy and the position of our planet within the solar system. Along with that there is information on the total population of the Earth, the average height of a human being, the structure of our DNA and the atomic numbers of carbon, hydrogen, oxygen, nitrogen and phosphorus – the elements we are made out of. No invading force in history has been given such vital intelligence.

American astronomer Frank Drake came up with an equation to estimate how many inhabitable planets there may be out there. He takes the lowest reasonable assumptions for the relevant factors. For example, he assumes that only one per cent of the billion stars in our galaxy have planets orbiting them – we already know this is a vast underestimate – and that one per cent of that one per cent are capable of sustaining life as we know it. Taking as a model the way that civilisations were eventually established on Earth, he worked out that, at the very least, there are forty planets in our galaxy with technology that is similar, if not vastly superior, to our own. And it would be those with a superior technology that would turn up on our doorstep – otherwise they would not be able to get here. They could, of course, be peaceful, fun-loving people. But think of the various civilisations that have grown up on this planet. The ones that flourished and took over the world were universally warlike.

And what happened when they came across peoples who were less technologically developed? They ruthlessly exploited and dominated them. Millions of people in both North and South America died because of their contact with a handful of technologically superior Europeans.

It goes without saying that any invading alien force that actually managed to reach the Earth is bound to possess technology far in advance of our own. Even in the unlikely event that they came from a planet orbiting the nearest neighbouring star, they would have travelled many billions of miles to get here. By comparison, the furthest the human race has managed to go is the half-a-million miles or so to the Moon and back.

The invaders will have had to master the fundamental forces of nature to get here. They will have some form of power that is beyond the imagination of humankind's finest minds. And they will be tough enough, physically and mentally, to survive a journey of billions of miles across the hostile environment of space. If it came to a shooting war, it would be no contest. Our puny weapons would be pitted against a technology that we could not even begin to understand.

Even if the aliens did not wipe us out on the first day just for the fun of it, or because they were so advanced that they considered us nothing more than lice on a disused planet, our governments would have no choice but to capitulate. There would, of course, be a few brave pockets of resistance, a handful of heroes who would rather live in freedom for one more day than face a lifetime of slavery. But they would not stand a chance. Humankind would have to accommodate the demands of the invaders or die. But what might those demands be?

We know that water is important. Although we know nothing of its existence outside the solar system, we known that it is a rare and precious commodity here. Liquid water exists in only one place that we know of – right here on planet Earth. Mercury and Venus are so hot that water boils instantly. There may be some ice around the Martian poles, but generally Mars has insufficient mass to hold water at its surface. The other planets are too cold, being made up mostly of huge balls of assorted gases orbited by a few lifeless rocky moons. But without water, life as we know it cannot exist. The aliens, when they get here, are likely to be very thirsty, so humankind could be in for a drought such as we have never experienced in history.

The invaders might also come to plunder the Earth's mineral deposits. The planet is still a rich storehouse of coal, gas and oil along with an abundant supply of diamonds, gold and other metals that aliens are likely to prize. Alien technology would make mining in places that were previously inaccessible a possibility. But they may need a workforce. That, unfortunately, is where we would come in. After all, to them, it would be simply a matter of pressing animals into service the way we do with horses, asses, oxen, elephants and water buffalo. In fact, these are the very animals the aliens might use. Humans are physically weaker, have greater difficulty following instructions and are generally more troublesome.

However, it might worth keeping some of the fitter and compliant humans alive to use as slave labour. There is nothing so alien about that. Until the beginnings of the fight again slavery at the end of the eighteenth century, every civilisation practised it. And in the twentieth century slave labour was used with ruthless efficiency in the Nazi and Soviet labour camps. Auschwitz survivor Primo Levi can give us some idea of what to expect. In his harrowing book, *If This Is a Man*, he writes: 'In less than ten minutes all the fit men had been collected together in a group... of all the others, more than five hundred in number, not one was living two days later.'

4 The UFOlogists

Stanton Friedman

Nuclear physicist Stanton Friedman is one of America's leading UFOlogists and has been research-ing the subject for over forty years, ever since a one-dollar book he bought in 1959 sparked his interest. He co-wrote *Crash at Corona* – the definitive study of the Roswell inci-dent –with Don Berliner. In *TOP*
SECRET/MAJIC, he investigated the Majestic-12 documents and US government efforts to conceal evidence of alien spacecraft from the American people. He has lectured around the world. He says that he silenced all but a handful of sceptics who refuse to believe that the Earth is being visited by intelligently controlled extrater-restrial spacecraft.

Curiously, Friedman has never seen a flying saucer himself. Instead he is a critical judge of other people's reports. Nevertheless, he says that seeing UFOs is much more common than most people imagine. At his lectures, he asks people whether they have seen a flying saucer. The hands go up reluctantly, he says, 'but they know I'm not going to laugh'. Typically, ten per cent of the audience admit to seeing a UFO. Then he asks how many of them reported it.

'I'm lucky if it's ten per cent of the ten per cent,' says Friedman. 'Sightings of flying saucers are common, reports are not.'

Friedman became interested in the world of UFOs by accident when he was twenty-four. He was ordering books by mail and needed to buy one more to avoid paying shipping charges. The one he chose was *The Report On Unidentified Flying Objects* by Air Force Captain Edward Ruppelt, former director of Project Blue Book. Friedman read the book and was intrigued. He figured that Ruppelt had to know what he was talking about. So he read fifteen more books on UFOs and spent a couple of years digging up as much information as he could.

His conclusion was that there was overwhelming evidence that Earth is being visited by intelligently controlled extraterrestrial spacecraft. However, he believed that, while some flying saucers are alien space ships, most are not. He believes that since July 1947, when two crashed saucers were recovered in New Mexico along with alien bodies, the government has back-engineered spacecraft of its own. Only a few insiders know that this has been done and he calls the cover-up the 'Cosmic Watergate'.

He began investigating the Roswell incident in 1978 after being put in touch with one of the witnesses. He has now interviewed over two hundred witnesses – of those some thirty were involved with the discovery and recovery of the alien craft and the subsequent cover-up of the two crashes. On top of that he has news cuttings from Chicago to the West Coast newspapers on 8 July 1947 and FBI memos that back the story. He also believes that these show that there was a second UFO crash in New Mexico in 1947, 150 miles to the west of Corona, the first crash site, in the plains around San Augustin. He has found eyewitnesses who saw 'a large metallic object' stuck in the ground there.

He is not convinced by Ray Santilli's alien autopsy film though, seeing nothing in it that was associated with a crashed saucer at Roswell or anywhere else. He is also concerned that Santilli has refused to have the film verified. Nor has he released details of the cameraman so that they can be checked out. Friedman likes to look at the evidence.

Friedman is not flattered by being called a UFOlogist. He says that it is supposed to mean a person who has studied the science of UFOlogy, but there are no standards.

'Anybody who reads two books and carries a briefcase thinks he qualifies,' he says.

A big part of the problem of proving that flying saucers really exist is that people make wild claims that cannot be substantiated by the evidence. But he is more annoyed at the failure of the media to do their job. They have failed to dig into what Friedman considers to be the biggest story of the millennium. He believes that the media pay too much attention to what he calls the 'noisy negativists', none of whose arguments stand up under careful scrutiny, he says. 'They sound good, until you look at the evidence and they collapse of their own weight.'

He points out that there have been five large-scale scientific studies on UFOs, ten doctoral theses have been published and hundreds of papers have been produced by scientists. But most people, especially the debunkers, seem to be totally ignorant of this enormous amount of information. In his lectures he goes through the five scientific studies and asks how many people have read them. Less than two per cent of these people, who are plainly interested in the topic, are familiar with even one of the studies.

Friedman is also invited to speak to government bodies and gets a good response. But he finds that the question-and-answer sessions with the government people are a one-way street. They ask him a lot of questions but they do not reveal anything. He has spoken at Los Alamos National Laboratory and pulled a huge crowd. He has also given testimony to Congressional hearings in 1968 and at the United Nations in 1978.

Friedman finds being trained as a scientist is very useful in his work as a UFOlogist. It has meant that his approach is objective, painstaking, honest and scientific. Much of what he worked on as a scientist was classified. He wrote classified documents and had a security clearance. This gave him the opportunity to find out how security works and was good training for searching government archives for classified material later. Now he now lives in Canada and works on less sensitive science research projects such as pollution control and food irradiation.

He believes that the Majestic-12 documents prove President Harry Truman set up a super-secret group of top people from the fields of science, the military and intelligence to learn about alien spacecraft. He has spent over twelve years trawling through fifteen government archives, checking out whether these documents are real. Repeatedly, he has found confirmation of details in the documents that no one but insiders could have known. Friedman has even collected $1,000 from one critic who claimed one of the type-faces used in one of the MJ-12 documents was wrong.

'It was an absurd challenge, since I'd spent weeks searching through the government archives and he hadn't,' says Friedman. 'It also typifies the intellectual bankruptcy of the pseudo-science of anti-UFOlogy. I've yet to see a good anti MJ-12 argument.'

Friedman has had no chance to check out the data on alien abductions, but believes that every abduction story should be taken on its own merits. He has faith in abduction researchers because of his dealings with them and thinks that some people have been abducted.

According to Friedman's theory the government used five major arguments for withholding evidence from the public. The first is that it wants to figure out how flying saucers work because they make wonderful weapons delivery and defence systems. Secondly, it needs to do this before any potential enemy does. Thirdly, if this information was released, the younger generation would see humankind merely as 'earthlings' – which is what we are from an alien point of view. Friedman thinks this would be a great benefit. The problem with that is that there is no government on earth that wants its citizens to owe their primary allegiance to the planet rather than their country. Fourthly, there are certain religious fundamentalists who maintain humankind is the only intelligent life in the universe – that means that UFOs must be the work of the devil. These fundamentalists have huge political influence and their religions would be destroyed if they were proved wrong. Fifth, any announcement that the aliens were here would cause panic. Some people would believe that the aliens were here to slaughter us. Others would reason that the aliens were obviously more technologically advanced than us and would bring with them new energy sources, new transportation systems, new computers and new communication systems. So the stock market would crash and there would be untold economic consequences.

However, Friedman still believes that the public is ready to hear the truth about UFOs. There would, of course, be some people who did not want to know – just as there are five per cent of the American public who do not believe that man has been to the moon. But the evidence about UFOs could be presented honestly and openly.

'I certainly don't think we should put technical data about flying saucers out on the table,' he says. 'But our planet is being visited by intelligent aliens. It's time we grew up.'

Jaques Vallee

Steven Spielberg's movie *Close Encounters of the Third Kind* made Jacques Vallee the most famous UFOlogist in the world. The François Truffaut character is based on the French researcher. Although he became a computer scientist for the Department of Defense, Vallee began his career as an astrophysicist. As a young man, it was curiosity that led him to study astronomy, but that same curiosity led him on into the world of UFOs. He does not find studying anomalous phenomena unscientific, pointing out that Nobel prize winner Niels Bohr said that all science starts with an anomaly.

He was working at the Paris Observatory when he first got interest in UFOs. They had observed a number of 'unidentified satellites'. However, when the scientists there were ordered to destroy the data concerning these 'anomalies' instead of sending it to their colleagues for further study, he rebelled.

This was during the early 1960s when the idea that UFOs were connected to alien intervention was widespread. Back then, he found that the 'extraterrestrial hypothesis' seemed to match witnesses' accounts. But since then, thousands more cases have been reported and statistical models could be used to analyse them. This has forced Vallee to take another, more critical look at the extraterrestrial hypothesis.

Vallee already had a passion for religious history, myths, occultism and parapsychology and, around 1968, he realised that many aspects of the UFO phenomenon were also present in the folklore of every culture. By 1975 he got the idea of combining these disciplines by considering the UFO phenomenon, not as simply a manifestation of extraterrestrial visitors, but as a control system that had been in existence since the beginning of humankind. He points out that UFO sightings did not start with Kenneth Arnold in 1947. Elements of the phenomena existed before. He believes that the wheels of Ezekiel, cherubim and burning bushes seen in Biblical times, the flying goblins in luminous chariots of the Middle Ages, the phantom airships of the nineteenth century, the 'ghost rockets' of 1946 and the extraterrestrial spacecraft seen today are all essentially the same phenomenon.

As we learn more about the history and geographical distribution of the phenomenon, the standard extraterrestrial hypothesis leads to glaring contradictions, Vallee says. He believes that objects and beings connected to the UFO phenomenon are symbolic, or even theatrical, manifestations, rather than a systematic alien exploration where abductions are conducted for the purposes of so-called 'biological studies', as other UFOlogists suggest.

'We are also looking at some form of non-human consciousness,' he says. 'However, one must be wary of concluding that we are dealing with an "extraterrestrial race".'

Vallee aims to shatter the assumption that 'UFO' means 'extraterrestrial spacecraft'. He believes that behind these enigmatic luminous phenomena is a form of intelligence capable of manipulating space-time and influencing human evolution. In his best-selling book *Confrontations*, published in 1990, he analysed over a hundred UFO encounters using scientific methods, and concludes that the aliens visiting us come from another dimension.

Vallee is the champion of a bold new speculative physics. He believes that objects capable of gradually appearing and disappearing on the spot are modifying space-time topology. This validates the multidimensional models of the universe that theoretical physicists have been working on in recent years.

But he does not totally reject the extraterrestrial hypothesis, just the hard-nosed American approach to it. He believes that we share our existence with other forms of consciousness that influence the topology of our environment and affect the human mind psychically. Vallee has been accused of contradicting himself, because at times he emphasises the physical and material aspects of UFOs, while at others stressing the psychic and paranormal side. But this contradiction is in the data, he says.

Vallee is a believer in alien abduction, but believes that hypnotising abductees as practised in America is unethical, unscientific and perhaps even dangerous. He has investigated over seventy abduction cases. From his interviews with witnesses he has no doubt that the large majority of abductees have had a close encounter with an object emitting electromagnetic radiation, pulsed at hyper-frequencies. The effects on the human brain of these are unknown, so hypnotising the victims could put them at risk. He points out that UFO encounters are dangerous enough to humans as it is, with large amounts of energy confined to a restricted space.

One of the abduction cases Vallee studied was that of Franck Fontaine, who was abducted on 26 November 1979 from the Parisian suburb of Cergy-Pontoise after seeing a bright light in the sky. Vallee was particularly interested in the case because he was born in Pontoise and went to the same school as Fontaine. Although Fontaine admitted, two years later, that the abduction was a hoax, Vallee does not believe the explanations that have been given. They do not correspond to his knowledge of the area or the psychological state of the witnesses.

'I don't believe it was a UFO, but I do think that Franck was actually abducted,' he says. 'Someone is hiding something.'

The dozen or so 'implants' he has examined have not been mysterious in nature. Analysis showed that many of them were the tips of rusty needles, fragments of insects or other natural material embedded in the flesh. However, Vallee was the first to draw attention to the subject of animal mutilations over twenty years ago in his book *La Grande Manipulation* ('The Great Manipulation'), but he has not published research because he was unable to prove the link between the mutilations and the UFO phenomenon. He does believe that the link exists, though.

Vallee finds the USAF's latest explanation of the Roswell incident – that it was the crash of a balloon carrying a basket full of mannequins – laughable.

'The most recent report from the Air Force is even more absurd than all the other "explanations" given previously,' he says. 'The fact that an extremely strange object came down near Roswell and that the military made every effort to discourage research into the incident and continues to do so is beyond doubt. However, this doesn't mean that the object in question was a UFO.'

For Vallee, the jury is still out on the Roswell incident. He believes that the idea of a crash is only plausible if you believe it to be a deliberate demonstration on the part of an external intelligence. In the meantime he is investigating nineteen other different crash cases.

Vallee believes that every country's armed forces uses the UFO phenomenon to cover up operations involving advanced or illegal weapons. This started in the USSR as early as 1967, when the KGB spread rumours about UFOs in a region where the inhabitants had seen rockets being launched that were carrying satellites in violation of international agreements. UFO rumours also cloak remotely controlled rigid airships that the military use to gather electromagnetic data. An American soldier he knows approached one of these craft standing in a clearing in Germany during manoeuvres before the Gulf War and he has read US patent applications describing them.

Generally Vallee's scientific colleagues are open-minded about UFOs. They have no time for grandiose conspiracy theories, but they do admit the existence of a 'non-standard phenomenon'. During his forty years of UFO investigations, he has discovered that the UFO phenomenon is considerably more complex than he used to think. It cannot be explained simply by an extrapolation of current human technology.

'We are faced with a phenomenon that underlies the whole of human history, manipulates the real world and seems to obey laws that bear no relationship to those we hitherto imagined,' he says. 'I believe we're entering a particularly exciting period in the phenomenon's history, since we now have the opportunity of re-examining all the various hypotheses.'

More recently, Vallee has published a memoir of his years in UFOlogy called *Science Interdite* ('Forbidden Science'). This also examines the validity of the US Army's secret 'Memorandum Pentacle'.

Bob Lazar

Soft-spoken physicist Bob Lazar is one of the most controversial figures in UFOlogy. A man with a strong scientific background, he has been involved in the 'back-engineering' of alien spacecraft at the notorious Area 51 in the Nevada desert.

In 1982 he was a member of a scientific team at the US military's Groom Dry Lake installation. There he worked on a top-secret project to unravel the technology used by alien spacecraft that had been recovered from various crashes. Nine disc-shaped craft were held under armed guard in an underground section of the base known as 'S4'. The job of Lazar's team was to find out what made these flying saucers tick and whether their components could be replicated with materials found on Earth.

Many people have poured scorn on Lazar's story since it was first aired in a TV interview in 1989. As a child he was eccentric. His resumé includes bankruptcy and an association with a Las Vegas brothel. Lazar is easily discredited. Officials at Area 51 deny that anyone named Robert Lazar ever worked there – just as they once denied that Area 51 itself existed. But a salary statement issued by the United States Department of Naval Intelligence proves that Lazar did work in Area 51 for the five months as he claimed.

And when it comes to engineering, it is plain that Lazar knows what he is talking about. He has an impressive list of technical qualifications and is a scientist with a pedigree. In the early 1980s he was employed on several projects at the Los Alamos National Laboratory, New Mexico, where the first atomic bomb was developed. At Los Alamos he conducted experiments with proton-scattering equipment and worked with high-energy particle accelerators. The work he did there was on the cutting edge of the new physics and could open the way to faster-than-light travel. As a prominent member of the town's scientific community, he earned himself an appearance on the front page of the *Los Alamos Monitor* when he installed a jet engine in a Honda CRX.

Despite the efforts made to paint him as slightly cracked, Lazar's account of what went on in Area 51 is lucid and concise, clearly not the ramblings of a disturbed mind. With his scientific background, his observations have a solid foundation. His specific task at Area 51 was to investigate the propulsion system of a small flying saucer dubbed 'the sports model', which was kept in one of the S4 hangars built into the side of a mountain. He witnessed a brief, low altitude test flight of the disc.

The sports model was some forty feet in diameter and fifteen feet high. It had three levels. The top level was an observation deck nine feet across, with portholes. Below that were the control consoles and seats, which were too small and too near the floor for adult humans to use comfortably. The main cabin had a headroom of just six feet. Also in the central level was an antimatter reactor and, located directly below it on the lower level, were the three 'gravity amplifiers', connected to the reactor by wave guides. He worked on this propulsion system both in situ in the craft and on the bench in the lab.

The power source for the sports model and the eight other discs in S4 was an 'antimatter reactor', Lazar says. These reactors were fuelled by an orange-coloured, super-heavy material called 'Element 115'. This mysterious element was the source of the 'Gravity A' wave as yet undiscovered by terrestrial science. It also provided the antimatter radiation required to power the saucer in interstellar flight.

The flying saucers in S4 have two modes of travel. For local travel, near the surface of a planet, they use their gravity generators to balance the planet's gravitational field and ride a Gravity A wave like a cork on the ocean. During interstellar travel, covering distances that would take aeons even travelling at close to the speed of light, the Gravity A wave from the nucleus of Element 115 is amplified. This bends space and time in the same way it is bent in the intense gravitational field generated by a black hole. As the saucer travels through space, time is 'bent' around the craft. By distorting space and time in this manner, the disc can travel across vast expanses of space at incredible speeds. This is the same principle used by the *USS Enterprise*'s 'warp drive' in *Star Trek*.

Terrestrial rockets push the craft towards their destination by blasting jets of hot gas in the opposite direct, while alien craft 'pull' the destination towards them. Lazar explains how this works with the analogy of a rubber sheet with a stone, representing the spacecraft, on it. To go to any particular destination, you pinch the rubber sheet at that point and pull it towards the stone. Then, when you let got, the rubber sheet springs back, pulling the stone – or spacecraft with it.

'In a spacecraft that can exert a tremendous gravitational field by itself,' he says, 'you could sit in any particular place, turn on the gravity generator, and actually warp space and time and "fold" it. By shutting that off, you'd click back and you'd be at a tremendous distance from where you started.'

Although this type of propulsion appears to be the stuff of science fiction, many scientists believe that faster-than-light travel may be possible. Cambridge University's Lucasian professor of mathematics Stephen Hawking has suggested that interstellar travel might be achievable via natural or manmade 'worm-holes' in the fabric of space-time. Understanding how this works in practice is a bit more taxing, of course.

Inside the flying saucers' antimatter reactor, Lazar says, Element 115 is transmuted into another esoteric material called 'Element 116'. This is highly unstable and decays, releasing antimatter. The antimatter then reacts with matter inside the reactor in a total annihilation reaction, where one hundred per cent of the matter–antimatter is converted into energy. This energy is used to amplify the Gravity A wave given off the Element 115 and the heat generated by reaction is converted to electricity via a solid state thermo-electric generator.

The alien craft were saucer-shaped to diffuse the electrical charges generated by the antimatter reactor. In flight, Lazar says, the bottom of the alien craft glowed blue and began to hiss like a high voltage charge does on a sphere.

'It's my impression that the reason that they're round and have no sharp edges is to contain the high voltage,' says Lazar. 'If you've seen a high voltage system's insulators, things are round or else you get a corona discharge.'

The craft's high voltage makes them hiss when they take off. Otherwise they are silent. And the hissing stops when they have climbed to twenty or thirty feet. 'There are just too many things that Lazar knew about the discs that can't be explained in any other way,' said George Knapp, the TV journalist who first interviewed him.

Lazar says that, at one time, there were Soviet scientists and mathematicians working at Area 51, alongside the Americans there. He did not know whether they were actually allowed to work on the alien craft, but believes that they were employed on the scientific and mathematical theory that underpinned his group's practical work.

They were kicked out after a major breakthrough had been made in understanding how the discs and their propulsion systems worked. They were none too happy about this. Lazar says that in the aftermath of their exclusion, paranoia at the base soared. Employees were issued with firearms, in case the Soviets tried to kidnap them.

During his time at Area 51, Lazar had to read a document the size of a telephone directory, which revealed that the top-secret base at Groom Lake was not the only US government facility back-engineering ET technology. The US government's admission that other secret bases do exist lent weight to Lazar's story. However, what goes on in them is still beyond top secret. Since Lazar's Area 51 security clearance was mysteriously revoked at the end of the 1980s, he has been subjected of intense harassment. His house and car have been broken into and he has been shot at by unseen snipers in an attempt to discourage him from divulging the secrets of S4.

Edgar Fouche

Like Bob Lazar, Edgar Fouche worked at Area 51 and has since spent his time telling the world about what is going on there. Fouche is a true insider who spent twenty-eight years with the US Air Force and Department of Defense. During that time, he was stationed at top-secret sites, including the nuclear test site in Nevada, the Nellis Test Range and the Groom Lake Air Base, home of Area 51. Fouche's work in intelligence, electronics, communications and a number of black programmes has given him inside information on some of America's most classified technological developments, including the super-secret SR-71 and SR-75 spy planes and the TR-3B, which many people believe is sometimes mistake for the 'Flying Triangle'.

However, during the 1980s when President Reagan was in power, he became completely disenchanted with the defence industry. It was full of fraud and abuse of power and he decided that he could not be associated with it anymore. He was suffering serious medical problems at the time and did not think he was going to live much longer. So he decided to speak up.

In this, he was helped by five friends who served with him in Vietnam. One was a former SR-71 spy plane pilot. Two of them went on to work for the National Security Agency. A fourth friend's father had worked for the NSA for twenty years and the fifth worked for the Department of Defense. He also gleaned information about the TR-3B by talking to pilots.

His buddy who was the SR-71 pilot told him that once, when he was flying back across the South China Sea, he saw a shadow fall across the cockpit. The aircraft started to nose down and the avionics went crazy. When he looked up to find out what was happening, he saw a UFO that was so big it completely blocked out the sun. It was oval and surrounded by a shimmering energy field, and he reckoned that it was three hundred feet across.

What really amazed Fouche was that all the pilots he spoke to reported encounters with UFOs. Some had seen circular UFOs, others had encountered plasma balls that seemed to dance around the craft. These reports were all the more impressive because the

SR-71 can fly at over 60,000 feet. This gives it enormous visibility. If something is up there, an SR-71 is going to see it.

Fouche's contacts told him that the development of the TR-3B started in 1982 as part of a top-secret project named 'Aurora', whose aim was to build and test advanced aerospace vehicles. He discovered that around 35 per cent of the US government's 'Star Wars' budget had been siphoned off to finance it. The TR-3B is a triangular nuclear-powered aerospace platform and is undoubtedly the most exotic aerospace programme in existence. Its designation 'TR' stands for tactical reconnaissance. This means the craft is designed to get to the target and stay there long enough pick up information on the enemy's deployment and send it back. The advantage of being powered by a nuclear reactor is that it can stay aloft for a long time without refuelling.

Its advanced propulsion system also allows it to hover silently for long periods. The circular crew compartment is located at the centre of TR-3B's triangular airframe. It is surrounded by a plasma-filled accelerator ring, called the Magnetic Field Disrupter, which generates a magnetic vortex and neutralises the pull of gravity. The MFD does not actually power the craft; what it does is effectively reduce its mass. Propulsion is achieved by three multimode gas-propelled thrusters mounted on each corner of the triangle. But MFD makes the aircraft incredibly light. It can fly at Mach 9 speeds vertically and horizontally, and can outmanoeuvre anything except UFOs.

One of Fouche's sources who worked on the TR-3B told him that they were working on the possibility of developing the MFD technology so that it not only reduces mass but also creates a force that repels gravity. This would give the TR-3B a propulsion system that would allow it to routinely fly to the Moon or Mars. This anti-gravity system is how UFOs work and Fouche is convinced that the TR-3B has been developed through the back-engineering of alien technology.

Fouche believes that the black triangles tracked by the Belgian Air Force in the late 1980s and early 1990s were TR-3Bs. He has a simple rule: if it is triangular it is terrestrial, if it is circular or tubular it is extraterrestrial. He says that the US government could easily get round treaty agreements that prohibit testing advanced aircraft over Europe. These agreements, he points out, say that they cannot fly an aircraft over a friendly country without that country being informed. It would be easy enough to inform the Belgian government on the sly. After all, the US is not supposed to have nuclear weapons in the UK or Japan, but they do.

Groom Lake's six-mile-long runway is the longest in the world. Fouche says that it was built to accommodate the CIA's latest super-hi-tech spy plane, the 'Penetrator' or SR-75; 'SR' stands for strategic reconnaissance. It can exceed Mach 7 with speeds of over 28,000 miles an hour at an altitude of 40,000 feet and can reach any point on the Earth within three hours. This plane is so secret that the US government does not even admit to its existence. After the SR-71 Blackbird was retired in 1990, the US Air Force said that it would not be replaced because satellites provided all the military's high-level reconnaissance needs. But Fouche's sources say that the SR-75 has been designed to service spy satellites in orbit. It acts as a 'mothership' and launches unmanned SR-74, or Scramp, craft. Operated by remote control, these can place satellites in space, reaching altitudes of 95 miles and speeds of 6,250 miles an hour, or Mach 15.

Fouche was assigned to Groom Lake in 1979 because he was one of the few people who had the necessary top-secret clearance. He was certified to work with particular equipment which, even years after the event, he was not prepared to discuss. He had been working at Nellis Air Force Base at the time and was told that he was being temporarily reassigned, but was given no idea of where he was going to be sent. Some thirty technicians were herded onto a blue bus with blacked-out windows. There were two guards on board, armed with M16 rifles. They told the passengers not to speak unless spoken to. This is how Fouche ended up at Groom Lake.

The conditions were extremely oppressive. He was issued with heavy glasses, like welders' goggles. These had thick lenses that blocked peripheral vision and prevented the wearer seeing further than thirty metres ahead. Everywhere he went, he was escorted by a soldier carrying an M16 who would never talk to him. He could not even go to the lavatory alone.

According to Fouche, the military used sinister mind-control techniques on employees. One of his five collaborators named Sal was a victim of this. A former NSA electronic intelligence expert, he had helped develop Magnetic Field Disruption. After two-years at a top-secret NSA facility, he came down with what he thought was the flu. He went to see the facility's doctor, who gave him some medication and told him to go home and rest. The next day, Sal had no memory of where he worked or who he worked for. When his brother contacted the NSA, he was told that Sal's contract had been terminated. Sal's memory has not returned and the only evidence he has that he worked at the NSA facility at all is a few scribbled notes and his pay slips.

Security at Area 51 was so tight that a key card and a code were needed for every door. Fouche is very sceptical about people who claim to have been at Groom Lake and accidentally stumbled into a hangar with a UFO inside. His twenty-eight years with the Department of Defense and the US Air Force taught him that anything that was top-secret was protected by numerous levels of security.

However, in Area 51 there is a facility on the Papoose Lake site called the Defense Advanced Research Center, which extends for ten storeys underground. It was built in the early 1980s with Strategic Defense Initiative money. The DARC is the centre for what is officially designated 'Foreign Artefacts' – this means alien artefacts. Crashed and recovered alien technology is stored there. The DARC is where all the analysis of 'extraterrestrial biological entities' – alien creatures – and back-engineering takes place.

Fouche says that the reason the US government cannot come clean about what they are up to at Area 51 is because, since the birth of the UFO phenomenon in 1947, it has consistently violated people's constitutional rights. The government considers anything that it cannot control a threat, he says. It cannot control the alien agenda, so it tries to control any information surrounding it. People who find out too much about UFOs or aliens either disappear or have been killed, he says. The government would be held accountable if the facts got out and it could not handle that.

David Adair

Another witness to what is going on at Area 51 is space scientist David Adair. He became involved in the world of UFOs through his lifelong passion for science and rocketry.

Adair was a child prodigy. He built his first rocket at the age of eleven. This was no fourth-of-July firework. He fashioned it from sophisticated alloys, using tools and fuels from his father's machine shop.

Then, in 1968, he set out to build a new type of rocket which used powerful electromagnetic fields to contain and harness the thermonuclear energy from a fusion reaction. Although this sounds exotic, it was not his original idea. He got the plans from the long-range planning division of NASA's Marshall Space Flight Center in Huntsville, Alabama. They had come up with the theoretical designs for fifty different types of engine. Only two of them used conventional liquid fuel or solid propellants, so fusion was the obvious the way to go. The one that Adair decided to build was a remarkable design. At the time he wondered why NASA had never made it themselves. Later he realised that they probably chose not to develop it for political reasons. If you developed an efficient fusion-based propulsion system, oil and gas would be redundant. Nevertheless the fourteen-year-old Adair saw the design's potential and, through Republican Congressman John Ashbrook, he got a $1-million grant to build it.

But the grant came with strings attached. The Department of Defense were involved. He was prohibited from telling anyone about what he was building. And for Adair the outside world ceased to exist as he worked on the rocket day and night for the next three years. In 1971, when Adair was seventeen, the rocket was ready to be tested. General Curtis LeMay, the project manager, decided that the rocket was too powerful to be tested outside a secure military facility, so he scheduled a test at White Sands

Missile Range in New Mexico.

When Adair was at White Sands preparing for the test, a black DC-9 arrived. It was carrying Dr Arthur Rudolph, one of the designers of the Saturn-5 moon rocket. Originally Rudolph had worked on the Nazi German V-2 programme, but after the war he had been taken to America. Adair told Rudolph that, proportionately, his rocket was a thousand times more powerful than the Saturn-5, and Rudolph was furious.

When Adair was programming his rocket's guidance system, his military bosses gave him a precise location for the landing. The coordinates they gave him specified a place four hundred miles away in an area called Groom Lake in Nevada. This puzzled Adair as all the maps showed there was an empty dry lakebed.

After the rocket was launched successfully, Adair was told to get on board the DC-9. They flew him to Groom Lake and, as they came in to land, he could see the huge runways and a huge base that had not appeared on the map. This, he was informed, was Area 51.

When he arrived at Groom Lake, Adair thought he was there to collect his rocket. But he was bundled onto an electric golf cart and driven over to three large hangars. As he got close to the buildings, he could see that they were new, but they had been painted to look much older. The middle hangar was the area of two football fields. Once he was inside, warning lights began flashing, guard rails sprang up and an area of the floor about seven hundred square foot started to descend. Adair realised they were on a huge lift. It went down through solid rock and, when it stopped, Adair found himself the biggest underground space he had ever seen. It contained a lot of aircraft. Most of them were covered up, but he recognised one as the XB-70, an experimental aircraft. It was huge. But he also noticed a number of craft that were a strange teardrop shape with their surfaces perfectly smooth in all directions. The most peculiar thing about them was that they did not have any of the intake or exhaust ports that are needed by jet engines. In fact, they had no visible means of propulsion, yet they were surrounded by support equipment and looked quite capable of flying. Looking back, he now thinks that they used some kind of electromagnetic or flux-field propulsion.

Still in the golf cart, he was driven over to a big set of doors. The driver jumped out and put his hand on a panel. It flashed and the doors opened. We know these things now as optical hand-print scanners, but in 1971 they were the stuff of science fiction. Inside the air was cold and the lighting was strange. There was plenty of light, but nothing seemed to cast a shadow. He was then shown a huge engine that was about the size of a bus. It looked like two octopuses linked together by their tentacles. When Adair examined it, he realised it was some kind of giant version of the motor in his rocket.

His companions explained that this engine used a fusion reaction similar the one he had designed and they wanted his opinion on the firing mechanism. The whole situation struck Adair as bizarre. Why didn't they ask the people who built it, he enquired. He was told they were on leave. So Adair asked to look at their design notes. This seemed to annoy the people who had brought him there.

'Look son, do you want to help your country or not?' they said.

Adair believes that the engine was extraterrestrial in origin. Although it was huge, he could not see a single bolt, rivet or screw holding it together. The surface was perfectly smooth and, although the room was cold, it felt warm to the touch. Whenever he touched the surface, bluish white waves swirled out from his hands and disappeared into the material. They would stop each time he moved his hand away. He climbed up on top of the engine and looked inside. He saw a large container holding bundles of tubes. These were filled with some kind of liquid. Adair's overall impression was that it was organic – part mechanical, part biological. He realised it had been made using non-terrestrial techniques and materials.

He shrugged his shoulders and told his companions that he had no idea how the thing worked. The manufacturing techniques used were very different from anything he had ever seen before. He reasoned that it could not have been built by American engineers or by the Soviets. As it dawned on him that it must have been built using extraterrestrial technology, he got angry. Flying saucers had landed and the government were keeping it a secret. When Adair expressed his outrage at this, his companions shouted at him to get away from the device.

Adair does not think that the engine was working too well, though they have had three decades to work on it since then and he hopes they have been successful. He could certainly see the potential. Adair's own rocket was puny by comparison but it channelled enormous amounts of energy out of the back of the rocket for propulsion. He believes that the alien engine could have managed to contain all the incredible energy generated by the fusion reaction inside the propulsion system, producing a 'field effect' outside the craft. This would create a huge 'gravitation well' which would break through the fabric of space-time. Space would be folded back on itself, allowing the craft to travel vast distances in an instant, without exceeding the speed of light.

However, he is still angry that this device and other exotic craft are in government hands and all their amazing technology is hidden from the rest of the world. Meanwhile people at NASA are struggling to send small spacecraft to Mars. The fact that the US government are withholding knowledge of their contact with other civilisations he also finds incredible.

'These are ET civilisations we could learn so much from,' Adair says. 'When I think of all the ways that we could advance with this knowledge of ET contact, it makes me sick that this information is hidden.'

Since his visit to Area 51 in 1971, Adair has worked as a technology transfer consultant, redesigning space-programme technology for commercial applications. He has an office in Ventura, California. But he has not forgotten what he saw.

On 9 April 1997, Adair testified to a Congressional hearing in Washington, D.C. as part of the campaign for full UFO disclosure. The hearings were organised by the Center for the Study of Extraterrestrial Intelligence and gave key witnesses, including military personnel and pilots, the opportunity to lobby the US government. David Adair was under oath when he told the Congressional panel what he had seen in Area 51 and, unexpectedly, the Congressmen immediately got confirmation that he was telling the truth.

During his testimony, Adair mentioned that the device he had seen was covering in strange markings. He remembered what they looked like and drew them for the panel. Also giving testimony was an attorney from North Carolina named Steven Lovekin, who had top-secret clearance when he worked as a cryptologist at the Pentagon in the 1950s. As a military aide, he had given regular briefings to President Eisenhower on UFO activity. In that capacity, he had been shown a piece of metal that he was told came from a downed flying saucer. It was covered in strange markings – the same markings Adair had seen in Area 51.

Wendelle Stevens

Wendelle Stevens' involvement with UFOs began in 1947 when he was assigned to the Air Technical Intelligence Center at Wright Field in Dayton, Ohio, home to the USAF's various in-house UFO study programmes, Sign, Grudge and Blue Book. That year, Stevens was sent from Ohio to Alaska to supervise a squadron of B-29 bombers that were being used to map the Arctic. However, he discovered there was a hidden agenda behind their polar mission. The B-29s were equipped with cutting-edge electronic detection technology and cameras to detect and film 'foo fighters', as UFOs were then known.

Stevens's security clearance was not high enough to allow him to see the footage the B-29s had shot before it was sent to Washington, but the pilots told him of their UFO encounters. Many of his pilots saw UFOs soar rapidly into the sky and fly off as the B-29s approached. In most cases, they caused electromagnetic disturbances to the plane's instrumentation, often affecting the engines. On one occasion a UFO approached a B-29 head on. Then, before they collided, it slammed into reverse, manoeuvred itself around next to the wing and stayed there.

Astounded by these revelations, Stevens asked his superiors if he could pursue an investigation into the UFO phenomenon. He was told he could do so only outside of official military channels. So, in 1963, after twenty-three years' active service, he retired and began a new career as a UFO researcher.

He began collecting newspaper clippings of UFOs from all over the world. Where photographs had been printed, he would write to the people who had taken them and ask for a copy. Now he boasts the world's largest collection of UFO photographs – over three thousand images in all – along with a vast library of UFO film and videos.

To establish the authenticity of the photographs, he visits the people who took them and investigates their encounter. He also examines their camera equipment and takes his own photographs from the same spot, so that he can compare relative scale and distances. After these preliminary checks, he subjects the photograph to a series of analytical procedures. Today he uses computer techniques. It was easier in the old days, he says, when all a photographic expert had to do was to make a large-scale blow-up and examine it with a magnifying glass.

Stevens is one of the few UFOlogists who had has made a career of studying contactees. In 1976, he was the first researcher to investigate the claims of Swiss contactee Eduard 'Billy' Meier, who was in telepathic contact with aliens and photographed their spaceships coming into land. At Stevens' behest, Meier submitted his evidence for analysis to scientists at McDonnell Douglas, IBM and NASA's Jet Propulsion Laboratory. Their results were inconclusive. However, computer analysis of one of Meier's pictures reveals a model next to a fake tree and models of flying saucers were found in Meier's home. Nonetheless, Stevens believes Meier is genuine.

Stevens decided to specialise in contactees because they presented a unique opportunity to learn about extraterrestrials and their possible agendas. If possible, he sets up a two-way dialogue, asking contactees to pose questions to the extraterrestrials for him next time they meet. Sometimes he gets an answer.

One of the most important contactee cases he investigated was that of Bill Herrmann, who lived in Charleston, South Carolina, near the Air Force base there. He and his wife repeatedly saw a UFO, which flew in a darting motion with sharp, angular turns, unlike the smooth turns of a plane. One night in 1977, when he was try to get a closer look at it through binoculars, Herrmann was abducted. He was enveloped in a beam of blue light, which drew him up inside the UFO. The extraterrestrials he encountered inside the craft were friendly. They came from one of the twin stars in the Reticulum system. When he asked them questions, he would hear their replies in English inside his head. They told him that the darting movements of their craft were made to avoid any radar lock-on. Radar-guided weapons had previously been responsible for the crashes of three of their ships. They also told Herrmann that they wanted their downed ships back and were prepared to negotiate, but the US government was too hostile to deal with. After this first abduction experience, Herrmann was invited back onto the craft another five times.

When Stevens began investigating the Herrmann case, he discovered that the Reticulans were sending Herrmann vast amounts of information when he was in a trance-like state. He transcribed the transmission in automatic writing. The result was numerous pages of text in a totally unknown alphabet, along with schematic diagrams of their propulsion system. The complex technical information he was provided with was way beyond current human scientific knowledge and Herrmann could never have acquired it from any terrestrial source.

From his work with contactees, Stevens has discovered that there are many different kinds of extraterrestrials. They come from different places and have different languages, morphologies, technologies and agendas. The largest group are the various humanoid species who often tell contactees that they come from the Pleiades star system. The next largest group are the well-known 'Greys', which again comprise a number of different races.

Stevens has also carried out research on Area 51 and tracked down Derek Hennesy, a former security guard who worked on level two of S4, the famous underground complex where Lazar had worked on alien propulsion systems. During his time there, Hennesy saw nine bays for flying saucer bays on level one. There were a further seven bays on level two with three identical alien craft in the first three bays. Hennesy also saw large tubes that contained the preserved bodies of dead Greys. After Stevens first interviewed Hennesy, Hennesy disappeared for a while. When he re-emerged he claimed to have no knowledge of what he had previously seen or said.

However, Stevens had another friend who works as an engineer at Area 51 and says it is engaged in bridging the gap between alien technology and our own. He has built simulators to train human pilots to fly flying saucers. There are two extraterrestrials at Area 51 who can fly alien craft. They have been trying to train humans to do this, but not very successfully. So far they are limited to flights within the atmosphere. They have not yet mastered flight in deep space, but they can hover using some kind of gravity propulsion.

Stevens thinks that there is little chance that the curtain of official secrecy surrounding UFOs will be lifted in the near future. The government have kept what they know a secret for fifty years and he expects them to do so for another fifty. Governments have far too much to lose from any official disclosure, he reckons. The impact on society would be incalculable. The only way the world's governments would admit to the reality of alien visitations is if a group of extraterrestrials makes its presence visible on a massive scale, he says. Stevens believes that there are signs that this may be about to occur in Mexico, where there was an explosion in the number of sightings in the 1990s.

Peter Gersten

For twenty years, New York criminal defence attorney Peter Gersten specialised in murder and drug cases. But then, in 1977, as the lawyer for the UFO group Ground Saucer Watch, he took the CIA to court and won. It was a historic victory for UFOlogy.

The suit was filed under the Freedom of Information Act. Ground Saucer Watch were trying to force the CIA to release just five UFO-related documents the agency had in its possession. But Gersten expanded the case. Under the FOIA it was as easy to create a lawsuit to get the CIA to release all the UFO document it had as it was to get just five. As a result, in 1979, the CIA was forced to release nine hundred pages of UFO-related documents – the first time that any US intelligence agency had ever released previously classified UFO information to the public. A further fifty-seven documents were withheld. But the case showed beyond any doubt that the CIA, which had previously denied any involvement in UFOs, had been studying them for years.

The documents not only confirmed the reality of UFOs and gave detailed descriptions of them, they also gave researchers access to numerous reports from credible witnesses – scientists, military personnel and law enforcement officers. Some of the documents released originated from other agencies. This confirmed that every other US agency had also been studying the UFO phenomenon and that the military had been involved in UFO research even before 1947.

Bolstered by this success, Gersten formed Citizens Against UFO Secrecy (CAUS), an organisation dedicated to breaking down the wall of secrecy surrounding the UFO phenomenon. Its aim is to force the government to come clean on what it knows about contact with extraterrestrial intelligence, and it believes that the public has the absolute and unconditional right to know.

In the early 1980s, Gersten continued his legal assault on the US intelligence community, taking the National Security Agency to court after the NSA refused an FOIA request for UFO-related documents that CAUS knew they had in their possession. In court, the judge asked the NSA's attorney how many documents had surfaced when they had processed the CAUS's FOIA request. He was told that it was classified information. Gersten told the judge that the CIA had told him that the NSA had at least eighteen documents. The judge then insisted that the NSA come up with a figure. The agency finally admitted that there were 135. But that was as far as it went. The NSA invoked the National Security Exemption, one of twelve exemption clauses built into the FOIA. To argue their exemption, the NSA used a twenty-one-page affidavit that was itself classified, and the case was dismissed.

Although Gersten was unsuccessful in obtaining the UFO documents, he did succeed in getting the NSA to admit that they held them. He took the appeal to the Supreme Court and, when it was dismissed, it made headline news. Even though he did not get the documents, he had succeeded in drawing great attention to the issue of UFO secrecy and highlighted the US Supreme Court's role in this cover-up.

In further court actions, Gersten succeed in forcing the release of a heavily censored version of the NSA exemption affidavit and, in due course, most of the documents they withheld have been released.

Gersten is not optimistic about the efforts of various organisations – such as Dr Steven Greer's Center for the Study Of Extraterrestrial Intelligence – to get US Congress to hold open hearings on the subject of UFOs. He says that the idea of open hearings is inherently ridiculous because any discussion of UFOs involves a discussion of advanced technology. This is an area that the military keeps secret by invoking national security, while the corporations protect their developments by using patents. The elected officials of Congress are always up for re-election – every two years for Representatives and six years for Senators. They need money and are always vulnerable to the demands of special interests.

Getting Congress to grant immunity to people who may have to break secrecy oaths to testify would not help. Gersten points out the problems: 'Let's say you have a general who wants to testify in a Congressional hearing even though he is sworn to secrecy. He will naturally expect Congress to grant him immunity. However, the military will then question Congress's right to grant immunity and they would then have to fight it out in the courts, which could take years.'

Gersten finds it more effective to work through CAUS where he can protect the privacy of any informant, through client–attorney privilege, at the same time getting the information out.

He used the Freedom of Information Act to try and pressurise the US Army into releasing documents relating to statements made by Colonel Philip J. Corso in his book, *The Day After Roswell*. Corso was willing to testify that he had seen the bodies of dead aliens in 1947 and that he had read alien autopsy reports in 1961. Gersten was ready to take the issue to court, so he filed an FOIA request with the US Army for the release of any documents they may have had supporting Corso's claims. The Army claimed it could find no documents and Gersten took them to court. But Corso died and, on 26 April 1999, the case was dismissed. Gersten decided not to take that matter any further. Instead he filed a suit against the Department of Defense over Flying Triangles, in an attempt to find out what these mysterious craft actually are. While Gersten concedes that some of the sighting reports clearly describe advanced US experimental aircraft such as the TR-3B, which researcher Ed Fouche claims was built at Area 51, many of the reports could not possibly be the TR-3B. People have seen triangular craft that are half-a-mile wide. Some are seen at treetop level and over populated areas, shining beams of light on the ground. Witnesses also report seeing orb-shaped lights detach from these craft, fly around and re-attach. None of this can be explained in terms of advanced military technology.

Gersten sued the US government for damages after Betty Cash, Vickie Landrum and her grandson were abducted in Texas on the night of 29 December 1980. Gersten argued that as the UFO concerned was escorted by twenty Chinook helicopters it must have been part of a military operation. The case was dismissed on the grounds that the government denied all knowledge of the UFO and Gersten could not prove that it belonged to them.

Gersten is also bringing an unprecedented FOIA lawsuit against the CIA, the FBI and Department of Defense on the grounds that alien abduction can be viewed legally as a form of invasion. Article 4, section 4 of the US Constitution requires that the Federal Government protect the individual states against invasion, a provision that was enacted to persuade the original colonies to abandon their independent militias and join the Union. However, the Federal government are plainly failing in their duty to protect citizens of the States if those citizens are being abducted.

CAUS and Gersten have even more ambitious plans. As it is unlikely that the President is likely to open up all the files on UFOs in the foreseeable future, they want to find out for themselves. They are planning a privately funded mission to the Moon, to send back pictures from the Sinu Medi regions where some UFOlogists have locateed alien structures. Using existing technology, they estimate that their 'Project Destination Moon' would cost $12 million – small change to the likes of Bill Gates and Ted Turner.

'Think of all the money sponsors would make from the publicity if they funded the first civilian mission to the Moon, especially if alien artefacts were discovered,' says the ever-optimistic Gersten. 'The space programme is in the hands of the government and the military. We are all like virtual prisoners on this planet. This is a project that is just waiting to happen.'

Derrel Sims

Alien implant expert Derrel Sims is a former CIA operative and got involved in UFO research after being abducted himself. He has conscious recollections of multiple abductions between the ages of three and seventeen. He started researching in this field at the age of sixteen and has been at it for more than twenty-seven years. After leaving the world of covert intelligence, he rose to become chief of investigation for the Houston-based Fund for Interactive Research and Space Technology. There he concentrated on collecting physical evidence, as he believes that this is the best way to prove that UFOs and alien abductions actually exist.

He has investigated hundreds of cases of alien implants, some of which have been inside the body for up to forty-one years. Despite being foreign bodies, they trigger no inflammatory response. He says that the devices found are 'meteoric' in origin. Although some labs have said that this is impossible, 'double blind' tests had proved this to be the case.

Dr Roger Leir

For years, people doubted the reality of alien abductions. This was largely because abductees had no physical evidence to back their stories. One man changed all that – Dr Roger Leir. A podiatrist from south California, he was the first doctor surgically to remove an alien implant. Until his first operation in August 1995, they had been seen only on X-rays and CAT scans.

Leir had a long interest in UFOs and was a long-standing member of the Mutual UFO Network, where he gained an investigator's certificate. As an investigator, he attended a UFO conference in Los Angeles in June 1995, when he met Derrel Sims. Sims showed Leir a number of X-rays. One of them showed a foreign object in the big toe of an abductee. Leir was sceptical, but Derrel produced the abductee's medical records, which showed that she had never had surgery on her foot. Leir offered to remove it and this led to a series of operations on abductees.

He selects candidates for surgery by strict criteria, which were developed when Leir was working at the National Institute for Discovery Science. Anyone undergoing surgery had to be a suspected abductee – they had to have experienced missing time or, at the very least, seen a UFO. They had to fill out a form that determined how deeply they were involved in the abduction phenomenon. They also had to have an object in their body that showed up on an X-ray, CAT scan or MRI.

Some of Leir's patients would have a conscious memory of the object being implanted into their bodies during the abduction. But, more often, implants are discovered by accident. Some abductees find unusual lumps and scars that have suddenly appeared and go to their doctors to get them X-rayed. In one case, an implant was discovered during treatment following a car crash.

All Leir's patients are given a psychological examination before and after the implant is removed. Some of them experience a newfound sense of freedom after surgery. One abductee went straight back to her family, saying she wanted nothing more to do with UFOs.

Leir has, so far, operated on eight individuals and removed a total of nine objects. Seven of them seem to be of extraterrestrial origin. Five were coated in a dark grey shiny membrane that was impossible to cut through even with a brand new surgical blade. One was T-shaped. Another three were greyish-white balls that were attached to an abnormal area of the skin. Leir found that patients would react violently if the object was touched and often suffered pain in that area in the week before the implant was surgically removed.

During surgery, Leir discovered that there was no inflammatory response in the flesh around the implant. He found this surprising as any foreign object introduced into the body usually causes an inflammatory response. In this case, there was no rejection. He also found that the surrounding tissue also contained large numbers of 'proprioceptors'. These are specialised nerve cells usually found in sensitive areas, such the finger tips, which sense temperature, pressure and touch. There was no medical reason for them to found where he found them, clustered around the implant. In two cases, Leir found 'scoop mark' lesions above the implants. In each case, Leir found that the tissue there suffered from a condition called 'solar elastosis'. This is caused by exposure to ultraviolet light, but it could not have been due to sunburn as only a tiny area was affected.

Leir found that the membrane surrounding the implants was composed of protein coagulum, hemosiderin granules – an iron pigment – and keratin. All these three substances are found naturally in the body. However, a search of the medical literature revealed that they had never been found together in combination before.

The implants themselves would fluoresce under ultraviolet light – usually green, but sometimes other colours. In one case, Leir found that an abductee had a pink stain on the palm of her hand. It could be removed temporarily, but would seep back under the skin. Derrel Sims uses this fluorescent staining, which cannot be removed by washing, to detect implants. Leir believes that it is caused by a substance given off by the implant to prevent rejection.

A wide range of tests have been carried out on the implants Leir has removed. They are submitted to routine pathology tests to see if they are human in origin. When that draws a blank, they are sent for metallurgical testing and they have been examined under optical microscopes and electron microscopes, and analysed using X-ray diffraction techniques that tell which elements they are made of.

When the T-shaped implant that Leir had removed from one patient was magnified one thousand times under an electron microscope, a tiny fishhook could be seen on one end of the crossbar of the T, which Leir believes anchored the implant to the flesh. The other end was rounded off like the nose of a bullet, while in the middle there was a tiny hole into which the shaft of the T fitted perfectly. One of the rods had a carbon core, which made it electrically conductive. The other had an iron core, which was magnetic. An attractive force between them made them cling together. The shaft was encircled by a band of silicate crystals. Bob Beckworth, an electrical engineer who works with Leir, likened this to an old-fashioned crystal set, where a quartz crystal and a copper wire were used to pick up a radio signal.

Specimens were sent to some of the most prestigious laboratories in North America – Los Alamos National Laboratories, New Mexico Tech and Toronto University, among others. The samples were found to contain rare elements in the same isotopic ratios that are found in meteorites. When the labs were told that the specimens had been removed from body tissue, they did not believe it. For Leir, this is the smoking gun.

When you mine an element on Earth, the ratio of the various radioactive isotopes it contains always falls within a certain range. If you mine uranium, for example, it will always contain a certain ratio of uranium 234, 235 and 236. This will be roughly the same anywhere on Earth. But rock samples from the moon or meteorites contain completely different isotopic ratios. The isotopic ratios in the implants showed clearly that they were not of earthly origin.

Leir is not sure what the implants are for. They could be transponders or locating devices that enable alien abductors to track those they have abducted. They might be designed to modify behaviour – some abductees exhibit unexplained compulsive behaviour. They might detect chemical changes caused by pollution, or be used to detect genetic changes in the body.

'If researchers such as Zachariah Sitchen are correct,' says Leir, 'and the human race is a genetically altered species, then it's possible that this genetic manipulation may still be going on and is something "they" wish to monitor closely.'

But whatever the implants are for, it is quite clear that they are extraterrestrial in origin. As Leir points out, if you find people who have been abducted by aliens and then find implants in them that have an isotopic ratio not found this planet, what other sane conclusion can you draw?

Tony Dodd

Ex-Sergeant Tony Dodd became interested in UFOs after having an encounter with one himself in 1978, when he was a police officer in North Yorkshire. He saw an object hovering about a hundred feet away. It had a domed top with four doors it. There were flashing lights around the sides, and three large spheres protruding from the underside. The whole structure was glowing bright white and it was silent. Dodd was sure this strange object was homing in on him, though it eventually floated off and landed nearby.

After he reported his sighting, his superiors told him not to talk to the press. This was standard procedure in the police.

Since then, he has seen seventy or eighty UFOs. Some of them are simply balls of light, anything from a couple of feet to thirty feet across. However, they seemed to contain some kind of mechanical device. He could often see a small, red pulse of light inside them, which created the aura of light. He has received had hundreds of reports of these balls of light, which apparently fly in formation. That must mean they have intelligent controls, he reasons.

After retiring from the police force, Dodd took the opportunity to speak out. He devoted himself to UFO research full-time and became Director of Investigative Services for Quest International, one of the world's leading UFO societies, and he oversees the publication of their high influential *UFO Magazine*. For part of his time in the police, he was a detective and he uses police investigation techniques on UFO cases. His police background has taught him which lines of enquiry to pursue and how to encourage witnesses to come forward and talk. It has also given him contacts in intelligence and the military. This is not always an advantage. Dodd's mail is tampered with, even the registered packages that turn up. And the CIA have threatened to kill him, though he remains stoically unintimidated.

Dodd is the foremost expert on animal mutilations in the UK and believes the government know all about it. He also believes that elite forces in America and Britain had adopted a hostile attitude towards a certain type of alien because the aliens out there do not resemble us very closely. Aliens, he points out, do not necessarily have two legs and two arms. Indeed, in human eyes some are quite grotesque. This is the reason the aliens are abducting people and creating hybrids. The aliens, apparently feel the same way about us. When people are abducted, they are treated the way we treat animals on game reserves.

Abductions are never one-off incidents, he says. Dodd has never come across a victim who has been abducted in childhood and never abducted again. Once it has happened, it tends to occur throughout the victim's life. Dodd believes that abductees are being conditioned until they reach puberty. After that the visitors start taking sperm and eggs. Part of the alien's agenda, Dodd believes, is a genetic experiment to create human–alien hybrids. He has investigated cases where aliens have impregnated female abductees. The conception is not natural. It is performed with a needle that it inserted through the navel. Human babies can be conceived using similar methods, but our medical profession is years behind. Three months into the pregnancy, the abductee is picked up again and the foetus is taken from the womb. The resulting 'star children' have thin limbs, large heads and alien eyes and faces, though they have hair on their heads and small human noses.

One woman he knows has been impregnated twice and both times the aliens have taken the baby. When the woman was three months pregnant, she was out walking her dog and a strange light appeared in the sky. She knew they had come to take her baby. She also saw jars containing embryos, which were suspended in liquid, as if in an artificial womb. These jars were all around the walls of the room she was in.

In many of the cases that Dodd has investigated, the abductees seem to have a sixth sense. They get a feeling when they know the abduction is about to take place. However, people generally do not know that they have been abducted. The clue is when they know things that they would not normally know about.

He uses lie detectors in his investigations. But he also uses his knowledge of the subject and his police background to sniff out the hoaxers. He also uses hypnosis and always employs the same hypnotist. This is because the man does nothing more than put the subject under hypnosis. Dodd himself asks all the questions. This is vital because he does not want the witnesses to be led or have them given guides or pointers.

In abduction cases, Dodd also looks for physical evidence. Some abductees have strange marks on their bodies. In one case he investigated, a woman saw strange balls of light in the bedroom at night, and she had an inexplicable burn mark on her arm. The woman had contacted him after he had made radio broadcast about alien abductions and, although many of the things he had mentioned had happened to her, she wanted to be reassured that she had not been abducted.

He has also come across a case where an abductee set off a camera flash near an alien implant in his head. Something under his skin glowed green. It was about a quarter of an inch wide, but it did not seem to cause the man any pain.

On several occasions, Dodd has had a person under hypnosis who has ended up speaking as somebody else – one of the aliens, Dodd believes. When he asked them what right they had to abduct people, the alien voice replied: 'We have every right to do this, you do not understand the nature of things.' Dodd concluded that he was talking to a highly intelligent being.

Dodd has tried to develop this as a method of communication with the alien race and has come to believe that extra-terrestrial beings are involved in a collect-and-analyse experiment to study the human race. He is in regular communication with them, but they only divulge things piece by piece. When he gets impatient, they tell him that they have to take things slowly because a human race is not able to handle the truth. We have to be educated as if we are in infant school. Dodd finds this very spiritual.

This is why they are not communicating with all of us. We are not ready for the knowledge they possess. That is why Dodd himself is here. His role is to disseminate information, to learn from the aliens and to give what he knows out to humankind. His alien contacts have told him that he is some form of teacher. Apparently this was decided before he arrived on Earth as a child and it is why they are making contact with him. They have explained humankind's place in the universe and have told him that we are immortal spirits that go on and on.

'Every flower has its seed and every creature its destiny,' Dodd has been told, 'weep not for those who have fulfilled their earthly obligation, but be happy that they have escaped that charge of material suffering. As the flower dies, the seed is born and so shall it be for all things.'

Dodd's contact with the aliens has religious aspects. He believes they are a higher force and that they are responsible for us being here.

A.J. Gevaerd

A. J. Gevaerd is Brazil's leading UFOlogist, editor of the country's only UFO publication, *UFO*, and the director of the Brazilian Centre for Flying Saucer Research, the largest organisation of its kind in the country. He came to international attention in 1996, through his investigation of the famous Varginha case, where two extraterrestrials were captured after their spacecraft crashed in southern Brazil.

According to Gevaerd, there were numerous UFO sightings in the first few weeks of 1996. On the night of 19 January, two people reported seeing a spacecraft which had difficulty flying. At around 7:30 a.m. on the morning of 20 January, a number of people in the town of Varginha reported spotting a humanoid creature around. It had red eyes, a reddish-brown coloured skin and three small bumps on its head. Frightened residents called the Fire Department. They located the creature in an area called Jardim Andere and called the Brazilian army. By 10:30 a.m., army personnel and firemen had managed to net the creature and placed it in a crate. They then took it to the School of the Sergeant of Arms in the nearby town of Tres Coracoes.

Gevaerd discovered that a second extraterrestrial was found

later that day. Three girls saw another creature cowering by a wall not far from where the first one had been captured. They told Gevaerd that it had a large head, brown skin, thick veins on its upper body and three protuberances on its head that looked like horns. At 8:30 p.m., a military vehicle with two policemen in it almost drove over a creature Gevaerd believes was the same as the one seen by the girls. One of the officers jumped out of the truck and grabbed it with his bare hands. He held it in his lap until they reached a nearby medical facility. Gevaerd discover that the creature was later transferred to the Humanitas Hospital in Varginha. The capture of the second creature occurred on a Saturday night when everyone was out on the streets. Many people saw the commotion and military trucks pulling up. In all, Gevaerd and his fellow researchers have interviewed over forty witnesses who saw the authorities capture the two creatures.

The aliens' UFO was first detected by an American satellite and the US informed the Brazilian military as part of an agreement between the two nations. So Brazilian radar was on full alert when the craft entered Brazilian airspace and it tracked the craft until it crashed into the state of Minas Gerais. Gevaerd has proof that both the US and the Brazilian government knew immediately that a UFO had crashed and knew roughly its location. Gevaerd tried to get details but there was a complete clamp down in the military. He believes that both extraterrestrials survived the crash, but died within a few hours of capture. The crash seems to have left them badly injured. The crash had occurred at around 3 a.m. When people saw them a few hours later, they were on their last legs.

'It could have been due to the crash,' says Gevaerd. 'Or perhaps the environment was not suitable.'

Gevaerd believes the US was involved from the start. He knows the creatures were later moved to the Hospital of Clinics at the University of Campinas. There were examined by a team of doctors, headed by Brazil's leading forensic scientist, Dr Furtunato Badan Palhares. In all, fifteen masked doctors examined the creatures' bodies, and seven of the team were non-Brazilians – probably US scientists. Gevaerd also thinks that the bodies were shipped to the US. A special US transport plane arrived on 26 January at Campinas, and he thinks that the bodies were taken to an Air Force base in North America.

'Everything indicates US involvement,' says Gevaerd. 'Our government does what it's told to do by the US. They co-operate with the US in return for favours.'

Since the Varginha incident, Gevaerd has consolidated his reputation by his investigation of 'Operation Saucer'. This began in 1977 when hundreds of UFO sightings came from an area along the Amazon river. Many people said they had been attacked by beams of light. Later many of them suffered symptoms of anaemia, although it is not clear whether this was due to loss of blood or to receiving a discharge from a UFO. The state authorities sent in teams of doctors, but they were attacked too. Eventually, the central government took the problem seriously, and, in September 1977, a team of twelve men from the Brazilian Air Force were sent to the area to investigate. They collected reports from over three thousand people who had seen UFOs and had been attacked by balls of light. This inquiry was called 'Operation Saucer' and was headed by Colonel Uyrange Hollanda, who told his story to Gevaerd in 1987, shortly before committing suicide.

The Operation Saucer team were ordered to talk to witnesses, document the evidence and get photographs – they took five hundred photographs of the UFOs in all. Hollanda's team were also ordered to see if they could make contact with the aliens and ask them why they had come. Although he got no direct answer to this question, Hollanda believed that the aliens were here to collect genetic material. Attacks usually took place when victims were alone and isolated. They would see a ball of light moving towards them. It would give them an electric shock, which would put them to sleep for several hours. When they regained consciousness, they would find small scars on their bodies, which Hollanda believed was caused by the extraction of tissue samples. But the damage was not just physical. Many victims suffered trauma and many were terrified. One fisherman who was attacked repeatedly was so terrified that he broke a leg while fleeing, Gevaerd says, but continued running despite his injury.

Hollanda reported seeing the craft associated with the attacks. They were sleek and teardrop-shaped with a large transparent area at the front, like a helicopter canopy, he told Gevaerd. On occasions, alien figures could be seen moving around inside. Towards the end of their investigations, short, humanoid, Grey aliens were regularly seen by the team. According to Gevaerd, the team's presence seemed to attract the interest of the extraterrestrials. Hollanda told Gevaerd that the aliens seemed to know everything the team did before they did it. For instance, if they decided to go up river, they would find the aliens waiting when they got there. Team members felt as though they were being observed. Eventually, the military team themselves fell victim to attacks. All members of the team were abducted. Hollanda himself was subjected to multiple abductions, during which he was examined both physically and psychologically by the aliens. He also told Gevaerd that he had acquired paranormal abilities as a result of his contacts.

However, these abductions caused Hollanda to lose his emotional stability. When Gevaerd interviewed him in July 1987, he broke down and wept. When he described his contact with the aliens he was obviously under great strain and was still plagued by strange phenomena years after he left the Amazon. He committed suicide two days before the first of a series of sessions of regressional hypnosis Gevaerd had arranged for him, thinking this might help.

Operation Saucer concluded that there was no doubt that the UFOs were responsible for the attacks. It also found that people were being abducted; some did not return. Gevaerd does not know why these abductions were happening, or why the aliens had such a special interest in the natives of the Amazon – although it is possible they conducted their experiments in this area because the people were isolated, living far from any protection.

Gevaerd finds the phenomenon of abduction a big puzzle. He has investigated cases where abductees have acquired paranormal abilities, including telepathic and healing powers, as a result. One case that Gevaerd investigated was that of Vera Lucia Guimaraes

Borges, who was abducted in the 1960s when she was a teenager. She was living in the house of her grandmother in Valencia, near Rio de Janeiro, when she was woken one night by a noise and was lured into the kitchen. There she was confronted by a ball of light, which hovered in front of her. She promptly fainted. After this incident, Borges acquired remarkable paranormal powers, including the ability to diagnose a patient's illness by simply thinking about it. Under regressional hypnosis, she discovered that she had been abducted by two aliens – one male and one female in appearance – who had subjected her to a medical examination.

Doctors were called in by Gevaerd to test her diagnostic skills. She was 99 per cent accurate. One of the doctors was so impressed that he used her as a consultant. In one case, she told him that a young male patient had been bitten by a poisonous creature and told him which antidote to use.

'I know of many cases where abductees have acquired paranormal abilities,' says Gevaerd. 'Although abductions appear to have no obvious benefits, there are plenty of cases that illustrate we are visited by ETs who can help us do special things.'

However, Hollanda certainly did not benefit from his abduction, and other abductees gain nothing and end up traumatised. Although there are a lot of dedicated UFO researchers in Brazil, only a few are investigating abductions. As a result, Gevaerd is collaborating with the North American alien abduction experts Budd Hopkins and Dr John Mack, who he hopes will teach Brazilian investigators how to do abduction research.

'There is so much new data here that has not yet been seized upon by the media,' says Gevaerd. He believes that it could be the clue to an enigma: 'I'm convinced humanity, in a number of different forms, is spread out all over the universe. We are just a tiny fraction of what exists.'

Jaime Maussan

Latin America is one of the world centres of UFO activity, and Mexican TV investigative journalist Jaime Maussan became interested when a huge wave of UFO sightings occurred in Mexico in

1991. He quickly became the country's leading UFOlogist. Since then he has gone on to investigate the semi-legendary, blood-sucking vampiric entity known as the Chupacabra, or 'goat-sucker'. These have attacked livestock throughout Mexico, leaving their carcasses drained of blood, and they are thought to be extraterrestrial in origin.

This first Chupacabra attack that Maussan investigated occurred on 17 July 1994. Official records that show that, around this time, people were going out into the mountains to search for a mysterious creature that had been seen sucking the blood from cattle. At that time the name 'Chupacabra' had not been coined. Maussan believes that this is important, because it shows that the attacks are a real phenomenon, not something created by the media. The media did not become interested until 1996.

Maussan's interest grew out of his UFO research. From the start they seemed to be related. When Chupacabra attacks started to happen, he began to look into them and soon found that they were a real phenomenon. This became his main area of research because it inspired even more fear in people than the UFOs.

His research has taken him to the places where the attacks have occurred and he has interviewed eyewitnesses. This led him to build up a network of investigators across the country and he corresponds with other researchers outside Mexico.

Chupacabras mostly attack sheep, sometimes chickens and goats. Rarely, they attack larger animals such as donkeys or cattle. But at least 80 per cent of the attacks Maussan has investigated were on sheep.

The animals concerned are domesticated and live close to humans. There have been no reports of attacks on deer or other large wild animals in Mexico, though Maussan has read a report of deer being attacked over the border in San Antonio. On that occasion, ten deer were attacked. However, even though they were wild animals, they were in a controlled situation. It seems that wild animals are somehow more protected from this kind of presence. Maybe they can escape and hide from the predator more easily.

The creatures in the first attacks were described as some sort of big cat with wings. The witnesses had all seen the creature close to, sometimes from just a few feet away. Then the press began reporting what was happening in Puerto Rico. In 1996 the name 'Chupacabras' was imported and hundreds of reports began.

The recent sightings are consistent. People are reporting an animal about three feet tall with a face like a kangaroo or a mouse. It has a small, spiny back, wings, little hands and very thick feet. Some people have seen it flying. Footprints have been found and samples of what appears to be the creature's excrement have been taken. Maussan's problem is that these incidents take place far out in the country where there are no facilities to carry out an investigation. When he finds out about an attack, it is usually two, three or even four days after it has happened. By then it is too late. You need to be there straight away, he says.

Rural communities are terrified of the attacks. In one town, local people painted crosses on the walls of the buildings around the site of the attack, hoping that they would given them some form of protection. After an incident in the town of Sinaloa, the whole community was so frightened that people could not sleep. There were so many attacks that people became afraid for their children. They figured that if the creature could attack animals with impunity their kids would be next. Animals were disappearing every night and people thought that it would soon take a child. They had to call in the army to get some protection. Interestingly, the attacks always took place at night. Maussan does not have any reports of attacks in Mexico that have happened during daylight.

Maussan has linked these attacks with UFO reports. Elements of the Chupacabra phenomenon suggest that creatures responsible for the attacks are coming from another world. Some people have suggested that they come from another dimension or reality. After having investigated this phenomenon, Maussan concludes that the creatures responsible are no known terrestrial species.

Humans have been attacked by Chupacabras both in Mexico and Puerto Rico. Maussan believes this may be related to the Mexican version of vampires. In Mexican folklore, people are turned into animals that suck blood from their victims. In one modern-day case a man managed to fight off a Chupacabra and escape. The struggle was witnessed by his wife and his brother. Their three accounts match. Apparently, the creature smelled very bad. The victim was left in a state of shock with two small, bloody holes in his arm.

To Maussan, this suggests that the same creature is responsible for old-fashion vampire tales and modern-day Chupacabra attacks.

'Perhaps these vampires were not human,' he says, 'and it is the same old creature that has been with us for a long time but we have never been able to discover exactly what it is.'

He has come across some cases where animals have survived for several hours after having been drained of blood. Maussan has found some strange substance left in the holes in the victims' carcasses which allows the blood to flow rather than coagulate normally. A proper chemical analysis of this substance might indicate what kind of creature is responsible for these attacks.

Maussan investigated the 1996 case, where there was an attack on some sheep in the small town of Puebla. A farmer, Dom Pedro, called the local vet, Soledad de la Pena. When she arrived she was amazed to see one of the sheep still alive, twelve hours after the attack, even though it had been drained of blood. Maussan thought this could be crucial.

'If we could find out what chemical was secreted to keep the animal alive after being drained of blood, it could be a very real and major breakthrough in medicine that could benefit mankind,' he says.

But Maussan has not been able to get this sort of work done in Mexico. Although some doctors and some universities have expressed an interest, none have come forward publicly.

Meanwhile, the authorities have been unable to explain these attacks, so they have chosen to ignore the whole phenomenon – another parallel with UFOs. And the church has refused to comment. Maussan is a little stumped about what to do next. When the Chupacabra attacks first started in Mexico, everyone was taken by surprise. By the time the media were interested, and Maussan had everything set up in order to investigate the attacks, the main spate was over. However, if the attacks start again, Maussan will be ready for them.

Dan Sherman

After twelve years in the US Air Force, Dan Sherman broke all his secrecy oaths and came forward to reveal his involvement in a super-secret National Security Agency training programme, aimed to teach him how to communicate with extraterrestrials. In just two years on the course, Sherman moved from basic extraterrestrial liaison to complex discussions concerning alien abductions.

Sherman's training began in 1992. He had been working in electronic intelligence analysis and was sent to NSA headquarters at Fort Meade, Maryland, for an intermediate electronic intelligence course, or so he thought. But when he arrived, he was told that he had been signed up to an extra training course in the evenings.

This course was part of a secret programme called 'Project Preserve Destiny'. Sherman was told that PPD had started in 1960. It was a 'genetic management' project and its purpose was to cultivate human offspring so that they would be able to communicate with the Grey-like extraterrestrials by a method they called 'intuitive communication or IC'. He was told that he and the other people chosen to work in the programme were the offspring of pregnant female abductees, whose foetuses were genetically modified during their abduction. As a genetically modified human, he already possessed the latent ability to communicate with aliens, but the course he was about to begin would heighten his IC abilities.

For ten weeks, every evening after his regular daytime training, Sherman was driven to an underground facility. There he was sat in front of a computer and trained as an 'intuitive communicator'. At the beginning of his training, he had to listen to a specific sound tone on headphones. Then he had to duplicate this tone by humming it mentally, while trying to affect the shape of a sine wave on the computer screen in front of him. This was made doubly difficult because there was no physical connection between him and the computer. Sherman believes that it must have been of a very advanced design that somehow picked up his brain wave. Anyway, after two days of trying he found he was able to flatten the sine wave.

After basic training, Sherman was moved 'PPD base 1', where

he went to work with two other officers inside a 'communication van'. The work seemed like any normal electronic intelligence operation, but while on duty he received his first extraterrestrial communication. He had just powered up his equipment, when a message came into his mind. It said: 'Prepare for information string.'

Sherman followed the procedure he had learned in training. Then after a few minutes, the alien communication began. It consisted of a string of numbers that meant nothing to him. But he typed them into his computer and sent them to the NSA for analysis. He was sure that the message came from an extraterrestrial intelligence, rather than some human psychic, because the means of communication was totally different from anything human. Psychic communication is often abstract and vague. This was clear and precise. Humans communicate in a linear mode, with a beginning and one thing coming after another until you reach the end. The alien data was non-linear. All the information was there in his head instantaneously. It was his job to interpret it and make it into a linear sequence, type it out and pass it on.

The communications would always be initiated by his alien contact, and would invariably be an array of digits. Occasionally, he would have to get the alien entity to repeat something, but essentially the communication was one-way. However, after three months, their mental communication began to broaden out. He was able to ask his contact a few questions. As he felt intuitively that the alien lacked emotion, he asked it whether it had feelings like we do. It replied that, although it had a similar emotional make-up, it was far less affected by its surroundings than we are. Beyond that, when he tried to pose more direct questions, the alien broke off communication.

Sherman was then transferred to 'PPD Base 2'. He continued to receive strings of numbers from an alien source, but he sensed his contact was a different alien being from the one he had been in contact with before. Gradually, the nature of the communication began to change. The strings of meaningless numbers became map references and they were accompanied by mental pictures. Some of the communication was launch data from unsuccessful US shuttle and rocket launches and he could see mental pictures of where the technology had malfunctioned.

After about nine months at PPD Base 2, Sherman began to receive information that he thought related to human abductions. Terms like 'residual pain level', 'body normalisation', and 'potentiality for recall' came up. His first abduction communication also carried a map reference, which specified a location in Florida.

Sherman discovered that this contact was a Grey. It told him that Greys had been visiting Earth for a very long time. They have communicated with various civilisations throughout human history, but this has been fraught with difficulties – hence the more diffident approach they are taking today. They had also visited a large number of extraterrestrial intelligences across the universe. Although their lifespan was similar to that of humans, they were not bound by space and time as we are. That meant they could travel huge distances across the universe by manipulating time.

As enlightening as this was, Sherman had begun to feel uncomfortable with his covert work. He grew tired of being told how important he was because of his IC abilities, while being treated like an underling with no 'need to know' what the communication he was handling was all about. He left PPD in December 1994, and quit the military altogether in April 1995.

After taking extensive legal advice, Sherman sat down with Area 51 researcher Glenn Campbell and wrote the book *Above Black*, about his experiences in the NSA's PPD programme. It was published in 1997. Since then Sherman has lectured at UFO conventions all over America and his story has been widely reported.

However, PPD is so far beyond top-secret – so far 'above black' – that it is almost impossible to verify its existence. Sherman compares security at this level to the layers of an onion. The outer skin is 'unclassified' – the activities the military get up to that the public see. Below that there is 'level five' which he describes as 'for official use only'. This prevents ordinarily confidential information being disseminated widely. Next comes 'level four'. This is secret information which, if leaked, would threaten national security.

'Level three' is top secret where information is compartmentalised and only accessible if the right codes are used. 'Level two' is a layer of black operations that only the US President and a handful of trusted Congressmen know about. Beyond that is 'level one' where 'grey matter' and 'slanted missions' such as PPD exist and where even base commanders may not know what is going on.

Sherman has produced certificates proving he was trained by the NSA in electronic intelligence to back his story. Other UFO researchers have checked out much of Sherman's story. But one – Bob Huff – has provided a whole raft of corroborating evidence.

A West Point graduate, Bob Huff retired from the US military to work as an expert in information technology in companies that were contracted to work for the Federal government and the intelligence community. He has also been investigating the military involvement in the UFO phenomenon for decades. Huff was able to verify that PPD Base 1 was the US Air Force Base in San Vito, Italy, and PPD Base 2 was Buckley AFB in Colorado. He was also been able to provide independent confirmation for the existence of PPD. One of his sources was a woman whose father was a senior marketing executive at the communications giant AT&T. He had worked on classified programmes for the intelligence community while at that company and was able to confirm the existence of PPD during a classified briefing.

Several of Huff's sources have confirmed that PPD was set up by Majestic-12, the presidential commission set up after the Roswell incident to keep the wraps on the subject of UFOs. He has confirmed that MJ-12 is in contact with at least one species of alien, either through live contact or remote communication. From what he has been told, you cannot apply to join a group like MJ-12. They never recruit. They operate by monitoring a potential candidate's career and if he fits their criteria they bring him into the programme. Huff believes this is what happened to Sherman.

'I think there has been an invisible hand guiding his career throughout his life,' says Huff.

Huff thinks that Sherman's strange method of communication is related to remote viewing – another project the military and intelligence establishments are pursuing. Both are paranormal channels and both operate on a non-local level beyond the normal constraints of space and time. According to Huff, Sherman is able to moderate some sort of 'paranormal continuum', so his modulations, in whatever dimension the aliens operate, are detected by their technology.

Huff has checked out Sherman's story exhaustively. Although he admits that, on face value, it sounds 'pretty far out', he has accumulated enough evidence to satisfy himself that Sherman is telling the truth. If so, this confirms what many researchers have long suspected: the military really is involved in alien abductions.

Patrick Harpur

Novelist and philosopher Patrick Harpur believes that UFOs are akin to fairies, the Loch Ness monster, Yetis, Bigfoot and many other inexplicable anomalies. They are the products of what he calls 'daimonic reality' – named for the Greek daimons, otherworldly entities who mediated between mankind and the gods. They inhabit a realm that co-exists with our everyday reality, as he explains in his book, *Daimonic Reality: Understanding Otherworld Encounters*.

Daimonic reality is an intermediate world between the material and spiritual worlds. The modern psychological concept of the unconscious is a recent model of daimonic reality. This places the nether world firmly inside us. But Harpur believes that daimonic reality is not really inside us, any more than it is outside us. In fact, it is impossible to locate with any precision. It is elusive, shapechanging and incomprehensible.

Nineteenth-century Romantics called it the 'imagination'. They experienced it as a dynamic realm separate from everyday reality, which was inhabited by archetypal images and myths. The Romantic imagination derives directly from the Neoplatonists' idea of 'Soul of the World'. This lay between the world we perceive with our senses and the ideal world of forms or archetypes.

The Swiss psychologist Carl Jung rediscovered this world and called it the 'collective unconscious'. At first, under the influence of Freudian psychoanalysis, he located it inside us. But later, when he studied religions and folklore from around the world, he was forced to recognise that it lay outside us as well.

'Reality,' says Harpur, 'is always psychic, lying between us and the world, partly inside, partly outside; partly personal, partly impersonal; partly material, partly immaterial, and so on – a reality that's as ambiguous as the daimons who personify it.'

Although UFOs are the most common modern manifestation of daimonic reality, Harpur says that people still encounter fairies. Although they are slightly old-fashioned, fairies are still around. They not reported because nobody is looking for them and people who do see them are too embarrassed to say so. Harpur wrote an article for *Country Living* magazine and invited people to write in if they had seen fairies. He received a sackful of letters. The creatures people had seen tended to be the little cherub-like entities of Victorian fairytales. No one reported seeing the classic fairies of central Europe, elves, or the *Sidhe* of Irish folklore. These were human-size and fierce, not little things with wings that sit around on flower petals.

Harpur points out that there are clear parallels between fairies and 'aliens'. It used to be fairies that abducted humans. They would steal young men to intermarry to improve their race and steal young mothers for their milk. This would now be interpreted as the alien agenda to produce human–alien hybrids. While fairies would pay us back by helping ensure the fertility of our crops and bringing us good luck in other ways, aliens provided us with a fertile crop of new technology.

Harpur believes that fairy wisdom has been 'literalised' into the aliens' advanced technology and finds the idea of delightful rural meetings with fairies more interesting than the grim exchanges that take place with the Grey aliens who bring humankind fear and pain. Harpur believes that the very sterility of the Greys reflects our own sterile view of the otherworld.

Harpur thinks that humankind needs its daimons, even today, when science tries to explain everything. This is because there has always been some form of daimon. Human beings seem to need some form of other-worldly beings to interact with. That is why, in an age when reason is supposed to prevail, half the world believes in flying saucers and aliens. You can't dispense with daimons. Being shapeshifters, if you try and get rid of them, they simply take another form. He thinks that it is crucial that we acknowledge daimonic reality. If we don't, the results are the same as if we seek to deny the urges of the unconscious. Freud formulated an inescapable psychological law – whatever is repressed simply reappears in another guise.

'This is as true of the daimons in the Neoplatonic Soul of the World as it is of today's unconscious complexes,' says Harpur.

The daimons always return. If you do not allow them in the outside world, they appear within as alien voices that cry out from the psychoanalyst's couch. And if you ban them from the world of nature, they come back from outer space.